Anonymus

Pious Practices

In honor of St. Ignatius of Loyola, founder of the Society of Jesus, enriched with

many indulgences by Pope Clement XIII

Anonymus

Pious Practices
In honor of St. Ignatius of Loyola, founder of the Society of Jesus, enriched with many indulgences by Pope Clement XIII

ISBN/EAN: 9783741163814

Manufactured in Europe, USA, Canada, Australia, Japa

Cover: Foto ©Thomas Meinert / pixelio.de

Manufactured and distributed by brebook publishing software
(www.brebook.com)

Anonymus

Pious Practices

PRACTICES.

IN HONOR OF

ST. IGNATIUS OF LOYOLA,

Founder of the Society of Jesus,

ENRICHED WITH

MANY INDULGENCES BY POPE CLEMENT XIII.

————◆————

COLLEGE OF THE SACRED HEART,
(JESUIT HOUSE OF STUDIES.)
WOODSTOCK, MD.

1881.

PREFACE.

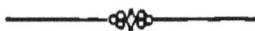

St. Ignatius of Loyola, the founder of the Society of Jesus, should be ranked among those apostolic men who have exercised the ministry of salvation and taught the principles of holiness.* Truly he was born to help men. God taught him much, and from these heavenly communications Ignatius composed his admirable book of Exercises. This work is exceedingly well fitted to direct souls in the paths of salvation and perfection.† The clients of this great Saint then look upon him as a mediator and a patron in the important matter of eternal salvation, and as a guide and pattern in the dangerous paths of the spiritual life. The

---

* St. Bern. fer. 3, in die. Apost.
† H. R. Rota, to Greg. XV.

virtues of Ignatius, therefore, which are here
proposed for meditation, will be arranged in accordance with the three degrees of the spiritual
life.   Hence, the Saint will be presented as a
bright model—first, in the purgative way; next, in
the illuminative ; and finally, in the unitive.   At
the end some considerations will be added on the
Saint's most precious death.   Each meditation
will be accompanied by a prayer to St. Ignatius,
three of his practical sayings, an example, a
practice, and an aspiration to be made frequently
during the day.   The meditations will be ten in
number, in memory of the ten months which St.
Ignatius spent at Manresa, amid great bodily
sufferings and heavenly joys of soul.   These
meditations can be used for the ten Sundays, or
for the nine days preceeding the Saint's feast ;
and for the feast itself, in order to secure his
powerful protection and obtain the grace to imitate, in some degree, his wonderful virtues.
The meditations will also serve to gain more
largely and surely the plenary indulgences, which

two Popes granted for the purpose of promoting and spreading devotion to St. Ignatius. By the brief "*Splendor Paternæ gloriæ*," our most holy Lord, Gregory XV., granted a plenary indulgence to all the faithful, who, on the feast of St. Ignatius, after confession and communion, shall pray for the Pope's intention in a church of the Society.

Clement XIII. graciously issued the following:

DECREE.

PLENARY indulgence of the ten Sundays in honor of St. Ignatius of Loyola, at the audience granted by the Holy Father, (January 27, 1767).

Moved by the humble prayer of Lawrence Ricci, General of the Society of Jesus, our most holy Lord, Clement XIII., kindly granted a plenary indulgence for all their sins to all the faithful, who, on ten consecutive Sundays before the feast of St. Ignatius, or on any other ten Sundays of the year, shall, with true repentance, confess their sins, go to communion,

PREFACE.

Christian works in honor of the said Saint, and
for the glory of God, and shall devoutly visit a
church of the Society. This indulgence can be
gained on any one of the ten Sundays. His
holiness willed that this favor should hold good
for all time to come.

Given at Rome, in the office of
the Secretary of the Sacred Congregation of Indulgences, on the
day and in the year of the afore-
said audience.

N. CARDINAL ANTONELLI,

S. BORGIA,

*Secretary to the Sacred Congregation
of Indulgences.*

DAILY PRACTICE.

1. MORNING and evening to do all our actions, direct all our affections in imitation of St. Ignatius. Offer them to God in union with the Saint's·affections and merits.

2. Say, in honor of St. Ignatius, ten *Our Fathers*, ten *Hail Marys* and ten *Glory be to the Fathers*, or at least *the Glory be to the Father* ten times to obtain some virtue. Say also the following Antiphon and prayer:

ANTIPHON.

I CAME to cast fire on the earth, and what will I but that it be kindled.

. V. The Lord hath led the just man by right ways.

R. And he hath shown him the Kingdom of God.

LET US PRAY.

O GOD, who to spread the glory of thy name, didst, through St. Ignatius, strengthen thy militant Church with new assistance, grant us that by his help and imitation of him, we may fight our spiritual enemies here on earth, and be crowned one day with him in heaven, who livest and reignest with the Father in union with the Holy Ghost, God forever and ever.   Amen.

3. Make the meditation, or at least read it attentively with what follows it.   Comply with the practice, and often during the day repeat the ejaculation.

FIRST MEDITATION.

PURGATIVE WAY.

St. Ignatius, a pattern of true conversion, by his ready, generous and lasting surrender of himself to God.

POINT I.—*Ready.*—St. Ignatius had already spent nearly thirty years of his life amid the splendor of courts or the pomp and circumstance of war. To prepare his soul to listen to the voice of grace, God allowed a cannon-ball, during the siege of Pampeluna, to speed on its way and break the right leg of the warrior. Confined to his bed by this event, Ignatius sought some means to while away the slow-moving hours. He asked for some of the light reading of those times ; but Providence so arranged that no book of the kind could be found in the house. In place of romances, his friends brought him a Life of Christ, and "Flowers from the Lives of the Saints." The reading of these works was the dawn of salvation for the sufferer. The grand virtues of the Saints stirred his soul to its inmost depths. By comparison he saw his own sins, and how good God had been towards him. A contest arose in his heart between

worldly pleasure and Christian virtue. Each
sought to win him to its own side. But said
Ignatius, if the Saints accomplished such wonders through the grace of God, why should not
I do as much with the same grace? Hereupon,
he resolved to change his life, to atone for his
sins, and to imitate the bright examples of the
saints. Full of this thought he rose from his
bed and threw himself on the ground. There
in that humble posture he gave himself wholly
to God, promising never more to seek anything
in this world except God and his glory. This
noble determination sent a shudder through hell
itself. The evil spirits shook the house of Ignatius as with an earthquake, and split open its
walls. Still, it was then for the first time that
the repentant soldier tasted true peace and joy of
soul.

Blessed is he who promptly answers the call
of God, and makes a full offering of himself to the
divine majesty. Had Ignatius disregarded the
voice of the Lord, he would not be honored now
among the chosen saints of heaven: perhaps he
would be in torments among the lost. People
make light of God's inspirations because they do
not consider the infinite goodness that sends
them, nor the infinite blessedness to which they
lead ; nor the infinite evil to which they expose

those who neglect them. "Thou knowest
not from whence he cometh or whither he
goeth."* You know not in what order God
intends to bestow on you his series of graces in
order that you may save your soul. Can you,
then, dare despise present graces, and promise
to yourself others in the future? What folly!
what rashness! "Dost thou know the order of
heaven, says God, and canst thou set down the
reason thereof on the earth?" †

POINT II.—*Generous.*—To give up the world,
riches, honors, one's home, to embrace Gospel
poverty, mortification of the flesh, and the greatest
self-contempt was now the firm resolution of Ignatius. Immediately God "gave him a strong
conflict that he might overcome." ‡ His elder
brother, seeing the wonderful change that had
taken place in Ignatius, suspected what he intended to do. He therefore appealed to Ignatius
in the most feeling manner. "I beg of you,"
said he with streaming eyes, "by our common
parents, by all our family interests, to look well
into what you are about to do. Do not adopt
any form of life that would brand the house of
Loyola with everlasting disgrace." On the other
hand, the evil spirit held up before his mind the

* John, 3, v. 8.   † Job, 38, v. 33.
‡ Wisdom, 10, v. 12.

mockery and scorn which the world would heap
upon him. People will attribute your new life
to cowardice, or to despair at the surrender of
Pampeluna. During this fearful conflict Ignatius
redoubled his prayers; he fasted, and, with many
tears, he sought God to help him. As in his first
danger, the Prince of the Apostles came to deliver
him, so now the Blessed Virgin, with her divine
Infant, appeared to him in order to strengthen
him in his holy purpose. This vision gave
Ignatius immense relief. It made an altogether
other man of him. In it he received such a gift
of chastity that until his dying day he never was
troubled with images or emotions contrary to the
lovely virtue of purity. Eager to show his gratitude to our Lady, Ignatius went to visit her
celebrated shrine, at Montserrat. Giving his rich
clothes to a poor man, he dressed himself in sack-
cloth and girded himself with a cord. Thus
attired, he entered the church, hung up his
sword at the Blessed Virgin's altar, and in accordance with knightly practice, spent the whole
night in watching and praying. It was the feast
of the Annunciation. Having made his confession, with extraordinary contrition, he went to
holy communion, bound himself by a vow of
perpetual chastity, gave himself again wholly to
God, and renewed his resolution to lead an
entirely different life.

Heroic magnanimity of Ignatius in overcome
ing so many difficulties, and in undertaking
such great and arduous things for God! We
are terrified by the slighest obstacles—a futile
human respect keeps us back. No wonder that
we make no progress in the ways of God. "The
sluggard willeth and willeth not. Every sluggard
is always in want. Desires kill the slothful ; for
his hands have refused to work at all. But he
that is just, will give, and will not cease." *

POINT III.—*Constant.*—Having once despised
the world, Ignatius guarded his heart with all care,
lest any dust of that world should stain, or adhere
to him. For eleven years he never asked his rela-
tives for any relief in his poverty, he never wrote
to them, and having once received a package
of letters from home, while he was at prayer, he
threw them unopened into the fire. Some
years after his conversion he fell very sick, and
was obliged to return to his country. Such was
his reputation for sanctity even then, that the
entire clergy came in a body to meet him ; but
as soon as he could escape, refusing the hospi-
tality of his relations, he betook himself to the
public hospital and began to beg his living.
Such virtue produced great fruits. Such crowds

---

* Proverbs, 13 and 20.

came to his instructions that no church could hold them. He was obliged to preach in the open fields ; people climbed trees, and got into every available spot to hear him. Many gave up their bad lives—dissensions were quelled—enmities disappeared—laws were made to promote public morality—many good works were begun and supported at the public expense.

Many reform their lives; but how easily they discontinue the undertaking! Whence this fickleness? Former bad passions and evil desires arise and entice. ·They are listened to. The heart is no longer s·raight before God : men become double-hearted before God, and are inconstant in their works. A double-minded man is inconstant in all his ways.* Wherefore "watch ye and pray that ye enter not into temptation."† For not he that shall only begin, "but he that shall persevere to the end, he shall be saved."‡

PRAYER.

St. Ignatius, model and patron of true conversion, the oblation which thou didst make of thyself to God with such promptness, magnanimity and perseverance, was the beginning and

---

* James 1, v. 8.   † Matth. 26, v. 41.
‡ Matth. 24, v. 13.

progress of thy wonderful sanctity. I who have rejected so many divine inspirations, who persevere so little in my purpose of a good life, and am like a reed agitated by the wind, tossed about by my disorderly affections, I fear lest my pusillanimity and inconstancy be the cause of my eternal ruin. How long shall I, dull of heart, resist the Holy Ghost that calls me? How long shall I take counsels in my soul.* How long shall I defer good works, or be inconstant in performing them? Help me, holy Ignatius, in imitation of thee, to begin, though late, to consecrate myself wholly and forever to God.

Relying on thy protection, I resolve and promise God that henceforward I shall seek nothing but him and his glory. O God! by the merits and intercession of St. Ignatius, confirm what thou hast wrought in me, that I may live faithful to thee unto death. Amen.

PRACTICAL MAXIMS OF ST. IGNATIUS.

1. THERE are very few who know what God would make of them, were they to deny themselves and give themselves into his hands, to be elaborated by his divine skill and industry. That you may rank in this small number, often say with your whole heart: "Lord what wilt thou

---

* Ps. 12, v. 2.

have me do?"* and do with the greatest care
whatever he shall bid you !

2. Though you have a prospect of doing much
hereafter for God, do not neglect to do now
what you can ; otherwise you may lose the one,
and not get the other.   Beware of this common
illusion.   "Whatsoever thy hand is able to do,
do it earnestly."†

3. In dangers we should not rely much on
the virtue of beginners.   It is like seed in Spring
time : it soon sprouts, but it also sometimes with-
ers away from mere contact with the soil.   Those
who at the entrance of the spiritual life do not
shun dangers prudently, quickly stray from the
right road.   "They became like the grass of
the housetops, which withered before it was '
ripe."‡

EXAMPLE.

THE apartment in the Castle of Loyola, in
which St. Ignatius renounced the world and
consecrated himself to God, was held in great
veneration, and in course of time it was changed
into a chapel on account of miracles obtained
there and through the piety of the Saint's own
family.   The number of persons who went there
on pilgrimages was very great, especially dur-

* Acts, 9, v. 6.   † Eccli. 9, v. 10.
‡ Isaiah, 37, v. 27.

ing the feast of the Saint and its octave. Sometimes there were more than fifteen thousand to
receive holy Communion in those eight days.—
Queen Mary, of Austria, the mother of Charles
II., to satisfy the devotion of the people as well
as her own toward the Saint, built a magnificent
church in his honor at Loyola, and enriched it
with many privileges and precious gifts. In that
church not only did many miraculously recover
their bodily health, but numberless conversions
were wrought and numberless spiritual favors
received. We mention here, briefly, two of the
latter. St. Ignatius there warned a man to confess five mortal sins, which, through negligence,
he had left out in a previous confession. The
man complied immediately. Another man who
had a bad memory, could not recall his sins.
He invoked St. Ignatius, and immediately the
man saw all his sins as distinctly as if they were
written out before his eyes.—*Bollandists for
July.*

PRACTICE.

In imitation of St. Ignatius, resign your will
to God—and always endeavor to do what is
pleasing to him.

EJACULATION.

THROUGH the intercession of St. Ignatius, confirm, O God, what thou hast wrought in us,

SECOND MEDITATION.

St. Ignatius, a pattern of true penance, in the chastisement of his body, in his interior mortification, and in watchfulness over his heart.

POINT I.—*In the chastisement of his body.*—Having overcome the world, St. Ignatius wished to unite himself more closely to Christ. He resolved, therefore, to conquer self, and first of all, to bring his body into subjection according to the words of the Apostle : "They that are Christ's, have crucified their flesh."* For this purpose he quitted Montserrat, and went to Manresa. Not far from this town he found a cavern, in which he took up his abode, and there he began his course of penance. Under the kind of sack that covered his body he wore an iron chain, haircloth, and thorns. Every day he begged his food from door to door. He fasted entire weeks on bread and water, except on Sundays, when he allowed himself some herbs or vegetables, which he sprinkled with ashes and clay. Every day, too, he scourged himself severely at least three times—he spent seven hours, one after the other, on his knees in prayer, and the little sleep he granted himself was taken on the bare ground.

---

* Galatians, 5, v. 24.

Once he abstained from food for three whole days; at another time he prolonged this fast to the seventh day—when he was found lying almost lifeless on the ground. People besought him to lessen this excessive austerity; but his answer was: let me at least suffer a little that I may attend to the important interests of my soul.

Take you, also, this advice for yourself. Suffer a little in this world in order to provide for the eternal salvation of your soul. Your past sins require this from you much more than from Ignatius: your present rebellious concupiscences call for the same. Endeavor to enable you to say with the Apostle: " I chastise my body, and bring it into subjection, lest I, myself, should become a castaway."*

Point II.—*Interior mortification.*—With the servants of Christ, bodily penance is employed as a means to subjugate the disorderly affections of the soul. " Those who are Christ's have crucified their flesh with the vices and concupiscences."† Wherefore, Ignatius, in accordance with the words of Christ: " If any man will come after me, let him deny himself."‡ In addition to corporal

---

* I. Cor. 9, v. 27　　† Galat. 5, v. 24.
‡ Luc. 9, v. 23.

austerities, he gave himself with the greatest zeal to the mortification of the soul.   In the first part of his life he was fond of the praises of men—he used to pay great attention to cleanliness and dress.   To punish himself for these defects, he concealed the nobility of his family; he took no care of his personal appearance; he mixed with the poorest and filthiest of men, and tried to imitate their manners.   He never combed his hair, and allowed his finger nails to grow immoderately.   Nor did he, while leading this horrid kind of life, grant his body anything that could please it or lessen its affliction.   Thus it was "he put away from him the love of self, and of all that is not God." *

Blessed is he, who by self-denial, has entirely cast off self-love, so that the love of God alone reigns in his heart.   It is vain to hope for a true love of God, unless we first drive out of our hearts all love of self.   You, who indulge yourself and all your desires; who see no fault in constant self-gratification; remember that if there is no fault now, there will be presently.   The devil is cheating you, and exulting at your behavior.— "If thou give to thy soul her desires, she will make thee a joy to thy enemies." †

---

* Process of his canonization.   † Eccli. 18, v. 31.

POINT III.—*Watchfulness over his heart.*—With
corporal mortification and interior self-denial
Ignatius joined the closest scrutiny of heart, in
order to pluck and root out of it every evil pro-
pensity. "It shall not leave them root nor
branch."* St. Ignatius was very remarkable for
this self-examination. At Manresa he began to
look into his conscience at noon and in the evening. He weighed all his words and thoughts; he
investigated their occasions and causes, whether
internal or external, with the minutest care.
Though he was thoroughly master of himself,
and merely lent, but never gave himself, to the
things of this world, yet such was his watchfulness over his heart that every hour he examined
his conscience. He learned from the Holy
Ghost another kind of examen, which he called
the particular examen. The practice of this examen consists of selecting a vice or defect that
we wish to get rid of, or a virtue that we intend to
acquire. Then early in the morning we resolve
to resist the vice during the day—we try to fore-
see the occasions in which we may be exposed
to fall, and we take our precautions against them·
—About noon we inquire how we have passed
the morning; we mark our faults on a paper

---

* Malach. 4, v. 1.

specially arranged for the particular examen, a model of which can be found in Fr. de Palma's little treatise on this exercise. Then we compare our examen, one day with another, to see our progress. We beg pardon for our failures, and renew our good resolution. In the evening, before retiring, we go through the same process. This exercise, when faithfully carried out, cannot fail to rid us of our defects. It is also an immense assistance for the acquisition of virtue. In this case, we choose the virtue which we intend to acquire; resolve on it, and examine ourselves about it, as above. But this exercise must be practised energetically. St. Ignatius never stopped until he had secured his virtue, or rooted out his defect. In this way he made daily progress in the interior life, and attained high perfection, and extreme purity of soul.

Whoso shuns this care of his conscience makes little account of spiritual progress. He loves sin; "he would not understand that he might do well."* Silly mortal ! when the time for judgment comes, there will be no room for correction, but only for damnation.† Endeavor, then, at present, by this twofold examination, namely the general and the particular,

---

* Ps. 35, v. 4.   † St. Austin.

to uproot and destroy every defect that is in thee. Build up, plant in thy soul all the virtues which, according to thy position in life, God requires of thee. "Let not your eye spare, nor be ye moved with pity."*

PRAYER.

Holy Ignatius ! admirable pattern of penance ! When I consider thy great bodily austerities, thy self-denial, and thy watchfulness over thy soul, I feel ashamed of myself, and I blame myself heartily for my contrary way of living. I seek pleasure as though I had committed no sin. I indulge my senses, my concupiscences that are the instruments and causes of so many offences against God. I am so blinded by my self-love that I take no thought of satisfying divine justice, to which I am so deeply in debt : rather I dare provoke that same justice by committing new sins. Oh holy patron I have pity on my soul I obtain for me from God, the true spirit of penance that I need so much, in order that I may bewail my sins, punish myself for them as I should, constantly deny my evil inclinations, watch always over my heart, and destroy the poisonous roots of sin, which still remain in my soul. Amen.

* Ezechiel, 9, v. 5.

MAXIMS.

1. BODILY mortification must not be so severe as to hinder greater good, nor so slight as to allow the flesh to grow insolent towards the spirit. In his additions to his Spiritual Exercises, St. Ignatius assigns the following four ends for bodily penance. First, to make some due atonement for our past sins. Secondly, to curb our present disorderly inclinations. Thirdly, to obtain graces from God. Lastly, to reproduce in ourselves Christ crucified. In these four ways then, under the direction of your spiritual guide, "bring forth fruits worthy of penance."*

2. We should value more the abnegation of our own will, than power to raise the dead. The latter belongs to what are called *gratiæ gratis datæ*, that is to say, graces which do not necessarily suppose personal sanctity in their possessor, and are given for the good of others. But self-conquest benefits us in this life as well as in the life to come.

3. To overcome our rebellious nature, it is good to enter into ourselves, and inquire what we have done, what we have to do, and what may happen us. Meanwhile we should be ready for the future. —Thus—"Set your heart upon your ways."†

---

* Luke 3, v. 9.   † Aggeus 1, v. 27.

EXAMPLE.

THERE can be no doubt that from his throne in heaven, St. Ignatius looks down with special love upon Manresa. There it is that he began his spiritual campaign ; there was his school of heavenly wisdom, the See of his primitive church, the witness of the many divine favors that God was pleased to confer upon his servant. The people of Manresa showed great charity to Ignatius whilst he lived among them ; and their descendants vie with their ancestors in piety toward their patron. Every spot that Ignatius had anything to do with is now sacred in the eyes of the Manresans. The cave in which he spent ten months has become famous. The earth and stones found in it are a cure for all diseases. Over the marble altar of that cave is a picture of Ignatius, in which he is represented as looking intently on the Blessed Virgin and her divine child, and learning, as it were, from them what he is to write. Beneath this picture is the following inscription : ‘‘Here St. Ignatius composed his Spiritual Exercises, which were afterwards approved by Pope Paul III.” Not far from the cave, in a church dedicated to our Lady, a bundle of sharp thorns, that the Saint used to wear around his body, is kept enclosed in his

silver statue. God has wrought many wonders
by these thorns. In an old hospital of the place
is a chapel that was once the room of Ignatius.
It was in this room that he had the ecstasy,
which lasted for eight days. Over the altar of
this chapel there is a painting of the Saint looking at the open heavens, and receiving from an
angel a banner inscribed with the name of Jesus.
— *Bollandists for July.*

PRACTICE.

BESIDES your general examen of conscience
for every evening, practice the particular examen
on any defect that you find yourself falling into
oftenest.

EJACULATION.

"PIERCE, thou, my flesh with thy fear,"* O
God, that I also may repent and do penance.

* Psalm 118, v. 120.

THIRD MEDITATION.

St. Ignatius, a pattern of endurance in his travels, in works of zeal, and under persecution

POINT I.—*In his travels.*—In an ecstasy, God made known to Ignatius that he had been chosen to carry the divine name to the nations, to kings, and to the sons of Israel ; and he showed the Saint how much he would have to suffer for the name of Jesus. Yet Ignatius received no distinct intimation of any suffering in particular. However, his great love for our Lord led him to Jerusalem with a view to bring unbelievers to the light of the gospel, or at least to win the martyr's crown. Worn to a skeleton with austerity, and relying alone on Divine Providence, he reached Palestine after many hardships on sea and on land. Several times he visited, with the deepest veneration and shedding many tears, the various spots hallowed by the footsteps of Christ, immortalized by his bitter sufferings, and consecrated by his blood. His soul overflowed with incredible sweetness while he was performing these pious pilgrimages, especially as our Lord himself often appeared to him at these times. He desired to spend the rest of his days in the holy places;—but he was unable to obtain leave from the

Ecclesiastical Superiors in Palestine to satisfy his
longing. With a heavy heart, and amid the same
perils at sea as formerly, he returned to Europe.
There he devoted himself entirely to spreading
the fire of divine love in the cities of Italy, Spain,
and France. Finally, at Paris, God bade him
present himself with his companions to the Sov
ereign Pontiff, and offer his own and their
services for the holy ministry, either among unbelievers, or in Christian countries.   The life
which Ignatius had led for so many years was so
laborious and so wretched in a human point of
view, that doctors of the Sorbon questioned
whether it were lawful for a nobleman to live in
such penury and abjection, even for the love of
God.   But the Saint knew well what he was
doing.   Our Lord often "showed himself to
him cheerfully in the way, and met him with all
providence." *

Perhaps we are afraid of the slightest labor
for our neighbor ; or to visit our Jesus Christ
in the tabernacle.   Yet we can undergo fatigue
for the sake of recreation and pleasure.   It is
only our steps for God that the angels reckon
in heaven : the others disappear altogether, or
they are numbered among our evil deeds, that

* Wisdom 6, v. 17.

we may be punished for them. Therefore, "make straight steps with your feet." *

POINT II.—*In works of zeal.*—As the Roman Rota observed, St. Ignatius did not consider himself the friend of Christ, unless he loved and cherished the souls that Christ redeemed. His zeal brought him a plentiful harvest of toil, of suffering, and of hatred on the part of men. When he was starting for Jerusalem, he saw that grievous sins were committed on board the ship: wherefore, he rebuked the lustful offenders with great force of language. These, conspiring with the sailors, resolved to abandon their troublesome monitor on some deserted island. Ignatius knew their intentions ; still, relying on God, he continued to chide the sinners. As they were nearing the island on which the Saint was to be abandoned, an adverse wind arose, and blew the vessel out to sea, so that his enemies had to carry him, against their will, as far as Cyprus.

There was in Barcelona a nunnery that Ignatius brought to repentance and a regular life.—This made some bad men of the place so angry that they gave him a beating, from the effects of which he was confined to his bed for three months. As soon as he recovered, he was again

---

* Heb. v. 21, 13.

at his works of charity.   His friends begged him
not to expose his life again : but his only answer
was : "Nothing better could happen to me than
to die for Christ and my neighbor."

At Paris there was a young man who led an
immoral life.   Ignatius wished to convert him.
One cold night in the depth of winter, Ignatius
plunged naked into a pond alongside the road
that the young man followed in going to his
pleasures.   As soon as he saw the young man
approach, he cried out to him in a deep, solemn
voice : "unfortunate man ! where are you going?
Do you see the sword of divine justice suspended
over your head ?   Go, enjoy your wicked delights.
I shall remain here in punishment for your sake,
until, by my suffering, I turn the wrath of heaven
away from you."   Struck by these unexpected
words, and by the great charity of Ignatius, the
young sinner was ashamed of himself.   He re-
traced his steps and gave up for ever his evil
habits.

"Recover thy neighbor according to thy power," * says the Holy Ghost.   "If any man have
not care of his own, and especially of those of
his house, he hath denied the faith, and is worse
than an infidel." †   But above all spare no pains

---

* Eccli. 29, v. 26.   † I Tim. 5, v. 8.

to recover the grace of God, if you have lost it; and avoid in future all occasions of sin. "Strive for justice for thy soul, and even unto death fight for justice." *

POINT III.—*In persecutions.*—The fervent exhortations of Ignatius, his holy life, touched many hearts. Remarkable changes of life, and conversions took place. These caused such a stir that Ignatius was looked upon as a sort of enchanter, or magician. People said that he bewitched men by his talk. He was often thrown into prison for this reason. However, his innocence was proved every time, and he was always honorably released. These trials did not prevent persons from crowding around him. He taught them the Christian doctrine and gave them some spiritual exercises. Some compassionated him at being put in jail. "Is a jail such a misery?" said Ignatius. "My greatest desire is to suffer for Christ, more jails, manacles, chains, and so forth, than there are in all Salamanca." A learned doctor hearing the Saint speak in this way, admired the greatness of his soul, and his eloquence; and when he reached his house his exclamation was: "I have seen Paul in fetters." Every conversion was for St. Ignatius a source of

---

* Eccli. 4, v. 33.

new suffering and persecution. On the other hand, new persecutions always brought him an increase of zeal and of spiritual joy.

Let us blush at our pusillanimity. Not only we cannot bear persecution for the defence of virtue and piety, but we cannot tolerate a slight mockery, a word of contempt. Human respect drives us from the path of duty. O, henceforth let us deem ourselves happy should it "be given to us for Christ not only to believe in him, but also to suffer for him." *

PRAYER.

MAGNANIMOUS St. Ignatius! I admire thy vehement desire to suffer for Christ, which no waters of labor or of persecution could extinguish. "Because thou wast acceptable to God it was necessary that temptation should prove thee." † Thou didst glory in tribulations, because thou wast "accounted worthy to suffer reproach for the name of Jesus." ‡ Faith teaches me what it taught thee, namely, that tribulations are a token of special love from God, and have for scope to make us like unto God's Son in this world, and in the next, sharers of his glory. My

---

* Philippians, 1, v. 29.   † Tobias, 12, v. 13.
‡ Acts, 5, v. 41.

lack of love for God is the reason why I find it
hard to suffer for Christ, why I shun the cross
or bear it grudgingly.   But if I refuse to be
Christ's companion in suffering, how can I presume
to share his society, and dwell one day with him
in his never-ending kingdom.   Wherefore, I
beseech and implore thee, Holy Patron, to obtain for me an ardent love for my God that in
imitation of thee " I may never glory, save in the
cross of our Lord Jesus Christ."*

Maxims.

1. When God gives one many occasions for
suffering, he is preparing that person for high
sanctity.   If, then, you wish to become very
holy, ask God to grant you such occasions.
"Because thou wast acceptable to God, it was
necessary that temptation should try thee," said
the angel to Tobias.

2. There is no fuel that so lights up the love
of God in a soul as the wood of the cross, which
Christ himself used at the sacrifice of his infinite
love.   If, therefore, thou desirest to love God,
"glory not, save in the cross of our Lord Jesus
Christ."

---

* Galatians, 6, v. 14.

3. He who fears the world too much, will never do anything notable for God. God alone is to be feared ; the judgments of the world should be despised. "If you had been of the world, the world would love its own ; but because you are not of the world, but I have choosen you out of the world, therefore the world hateth you." *

EXAMPLE.

WHILE Ignatius was ardently laboring for the good of souls at Barcelona, without the slightest fear, though persons there had carried their violence towards him so far as even to beat him severely, an event took place that made his holiness very conspicuous. Two brothers were at law about an inheritance: judgment was given. The one who lost the suit was so overwhelmed with grief and despair that, in a moment of strong temptation, he hanged himself in his own room. The neighbors came in crowds to see the horrid sight. As soon as he heard what had happened, Ignatius too, ran to the house, cut down the dead body, and ordered it to be laid on the bed. Then falling on his knees, he prayed to God with many tears, for the salvation of that unfortunate soul.

---

* John, 15, v. 19.

Wonderful to say! while Ignatius prayed, and all eyes were riveted in expectation on the corpse, the wretched man opened his eyes, called for a priest, made his confession, and then gave up his soul to God. This miracle was reported throughout the town and all over the country, and it excited everywhere the greatest admiration for Ignatius.—*Bollandists for July.*

PRACTICE.

PATIENCE in adversity. Patience hath a perfect work.*

EJACULATION.

MAY I never glory, save in the cross of our Lord Jesus Christ.

---

* James, I, v. 4.

FOURTH MEDITATION.

THE ILLUMINATIVE WAY.

St. Ignatius a pattern of prayer in his application to prayer, in the gift of contemplation, and in the teaching of prayer.

POINT I.—*In application to prayer.*—The immense zeal which St. Ignatius felt for Christ and his glory, was lit up in his soul by his application to prayer. At the beginning of his conversion he did himself much violence for the sake of prayer. He remained seven hours every day on his knees in prayer. Gradually, through the assistance of God, he released himself from subjection to the body, and then he attained such a gift of prayer that as soon as he placed himself in the divine presence, he was rapt up in God, his heart glowed as in a fire, and his face was all ablaze "from the conversation of the Lord."* During the whole day he felt such sweetness of soul, he was so lost in God that a look at the heavens, at the stars, on which he loved to gaze, the sight of a flower, or of any object in nature, no matter how trifling, spoke to him of God,

---

* Exod. 34, v. 29.

filled his soul with delight, and absorbed him in divine love. He undertook nothing of any consequence, before consulting and begging the favor of God. The slightest religious duty filled him with an ardor that appeared exteriorly, glowed in his eyes, and made him burst into tears. Indeed, he wept so much in this way that he injured his eyesight very seriously. Yet the loss did not affect him in the least. His friends, however, prevailed on him to ask God for power to restrain his weeping. The prayer was heard, for ever afterwards he had such a mastery over his tears that he could withhold, or let them flow at will.

Would that we had the habit of seeing God's power, wisdom, and goodness in every created object. This gift is obtained only by persevering prayer. We pray heedlessly, our thoughts, our hearts wander ; so that our Lord may say to us : "What ! could you not watch one hour with me ? Watch ye, and pray that ye enter not into temptation."*

Point II.— *The gift of contemplation.*— By continually devoting himself to prayer, Ignatius attained the highest excellence in that holy exercise. He frankly avowed that at Manresa he

* Matth. 26, v. 40-41.

learned more from God in an hour, than all the
learned men of the world could teach him.
During his contemplations in that blessed retreat,
he was often rapt in ecstasy. He saw our Lord
most clearly in the Sacred Host: he gained a
profound insight into the Incarnation, and other
Christian mysteries. When he recited the Creed,
the adorable Trinity, three in persons one in
essence, was manifest to him, so that he, a man
of no learning, did not hesitate to write a book
on that most august mystery. These visions so
strengthened Ignatius in the true faith that were
there no other proofs of Christianity, he would
not have hesitated to die for it merely on account
of what God taught him at Manresa. In those
raptures, which at times lasted from two even to
eight days, his countenance was lit up, rays of
light encircled his head, and his body was raised
from the ground. During them our Lord and
the Blessed Virgin appeared visibly to him, and
gave him instructions. Ever after this period
of his life, Ignatius enjoyed such union and
familiarity with God that those who knew him
intimately, considered his existence as an un-
broken contemplation and one uninterrupted
ecstasy.* Yet though possessing so high a

* James Alvarez de Paz, De vita Spir. Tom 3, lib.
2, c. 3.

degree of contemplation, whenever he intended to pray, he prepared himself with as much care as if he were wholly unpractised.

How different is our way of acting in this regard ! We go to prayer without any preparation, and full of distractions. What wonder that our minds wander as long as our prayer lasts. Before prayer or meditation, let us bring to mind the subject upon which we are about to meditate, or to pray. When praying we should place ourselves before God with great faith and eargerness, and ask him "to cause the light of his countenance to shine on us." * We should also watch, and keep our mind from running to other thoughts. "Before prayer, prepare thy soul : and be not as a man that tempteth God."†

POINT III.—*Teaching prayer.*— God choose St. Ignatius for the gaining of many souls, and to direct them, mainly by his Spiritual Exercises, in the way of salvation and perfection. Hence, he led his servant through all the arduous paths . of the spiritual life ; he allowed him to be afflicted with every form of scruple and temptation, so that he might learn, by his own personal experience, the heavenly art of guiding souls amid those dark and dangerous regions. At a later

---

* Ps. 66, v. 2.   † Eccli 18, v. 23.

period, St. Ignatius looked back on the origin and
stages of his conversion ; he reviewed its various
storms of temptation, and the serenity that came
after them ; and from what he there learned from
God, or from his own experience, he wrote out
instructions for praying and meditating with
profit to the soul. In the course of time he
enlarged this work, adding to it many useful
observations and directions, and he finally gave
it to the world under the title of *" Spiritual
Exercises."* It received the full approbation of the
Holy See. The book has been of the greatest
assistance to people of every age and class in
society for the choice of a state of life, for their
advancement in the Christian life and their perseverance in virtue. The Exercises of St. Ignatius
are looked upon as one of the chief means that
God has employed to correct the vices of the
world, and bring back the children of the church
to primitive fervor and discipline. Many would
wish to acquire the science of the saints, but at
no cost to themselves. Vain desire ! No one
ever learnt that science, until he did himself
violence, and practised what he intended to
learn. Nearly all the holy men that have lived
since the time of St. Ignatius found in his
Spiritual Exercises "that hidden manna which

no man knoweth, but he that receiveth it."*
Would that you also would listen to the divine
voice, and enter the solitude of the Exercises to
hear the same voice more distinctly.   Then, the
Holy Spirit would speak to your heart, and
teach you whatever is necessary for your salvation
and perfection.   "Come ye to him and be enlightened.   O taste and see that the Lord is
sweet." †

PRAYER.

HOLY patriarch Ignatius ! So admirable in the
practice and teaching of prayer, and for thy gift
of contemplation, look at my heart.   It is dull,
heavy, weighed down with earthly affections, because, though God has invited me many times, I
have neglected to devote myself to prayer, that
fountain of every grace.   My cowardliness, my
ungratefulness to God, deserve that he should
drive me from his face, that he should hide that
glorious face from me, since I have not known
the day of my visitation.   O holy patron ! beg
pardon of God for me.   Beseech him not to turn
away his face from me, or to hide his light from
my eyes, but rather to have mercy on me and
shed the light of his countenance upon me, when
I pray.   I resolve to devote every day a certain

---

* Apocal. 2, v. 17.   † Ps. 33, v. 6 9.

time to prayer, to raise my heart to God by frequent aspirations in the course of the day—that
in imitation of thee, I may always be united with
God on earth, and, through thy intercession,
merit to enjoy him for ever in heaven. Amen.

MAXIMS.

1. By meditating carefully and diligently on
eternal truths, we can easily overcome the various
inclinations to evil in which our corrupt nature
abounds. If you do not experience this facility,
blame your negligence in meditation, and correct
it, "I have thought on my ways; and turned my
feet unto thy testimonies."*

2. He, who in everything that he does, constantly keeps God before his eyes, will not feel
. less devotion in works of charity and obedience
than in prayer itself. Accustom yourself to this
exercise of the presence of God, and your heart
will rejoice; "I set the Lord always in my sight,
Therefore, my heart hath been glad."†

3. Grant me, O my God, the gift of true
humility and of loving reverence in thy sight.
This was a common aspiration with St. Ignatius.
By it he constantly kept up an affectionate presence of God. "Let us humble our souls before

---

* Ps. 118, v. 59.　　† Ps. 15, v. 8–9.

the Lord God and continue in an humble spirit
in his service."*

EXAMPLE.

WHILE Ignatius was going through his studies
he lost no opportunity to gain souls to God by
his Exercises. The following fact is a proof of his
zeal at that time. Once, in Paris, a nobleman
invited him, in fun, to play some game with him.
"I shall play with you," said Ignatius. "But what
are to be the stakes," said the nobleman, "since
you have no money?" "The stakes will be," answered Ignatius, "that if you win, I shall serve you
for a certain number of days in whatever way
you choose; but if I win, you will serve me as I
please." "Agreed," said the nobleman. They
began the game. Ignatius knew nothing at all
about it; still, with the help of God he won at
every turn. "I am duly punished for challenging
you," said the nobleman; "God is against me."
When the game was over, Ignatius took the
loser, gave him the Spiritual Exercises for a few
days, and out of a man addicted only to sloth and
worldly pleasures, he made an earnest Christian
that feared God, and prepared for eternity.—*Bollandists for July.*

---

* Judith. 8, v. 16.

PRACTICE.

WHEN you go to pray, place yourself in God's prensece, and do not allow your mind to wander away to other things.

EJACULATION.

" LET my supplication, O Lord, come near in thy sight, give me understanding according to thy word."*

FIFTH MEDITATION.

St. Ignatius, the pattern of true humility in his knowledge of himself, in his love for humiliation, and in his heavenly gifts.

POINT I.—*In his knowledge of himself.*—Interior humility consists in an abiding sense of our own nothingness, and in a love for everything that can lead us to contemn ourselves. This is the definition, which, by order of the Blessed Virgin, St. Ignatius gave of that virtue when he appeared to

* Ps. 118, v. 169.

St. Mary Magdalen of Pazzi. In order that he himself might reach this knowledge of his own nothingness, he looked upon all his gifts in the order of nature and of grace, as so many favors done by God to an ungrateful man. He claimed as his own, only nothingness, ignorance, error; a fountain of sin, and many actual sins. Thinking thus humbly of himself, he contrasted himself, first, with all mankind; then, with the countless multitudes of magnificent angels, and with the infinite majesty of God. What are all creatures, he would exclaim, when put alongside of the Creator? "All nations are before God as if they had no being at all, and are counted to him as nothing and vanity." * How little I am, then, before God! What am I in his sight except dust and ashes, corruption and worms, whether I consider the loathsomeness of my body, or the foulness of my soul, from which so many sins and vices are constantly oozing! These were the humble sentiments that he entertained of himself, and of all that belonged to him. In his own eyes he deserved nothing but contempt, hatred, humiliation, and all manner of chastisement. He thought himself the least of mankind, and the greatest pauper with respect to everything good and holy.

You, who make so much of your talents and
deeds, what have you that you did not receive?
And if you have received, why do you glory as
though you had not received it? *   "Thy arro-
gance have deceived thee and the pride of thy
heart."† Separate every precious gift of God from
your original and vile nothingness, from your
moral depravity, and you will clearly see with
what good right God can say to you: " Behold I
have made thee a little one among the nations,
very despicable among men."‡

POINT II.—*The love of humiliations.*—St. Ignatius
laid down this law for himself which agrees
so well with his very low estimate of himself,
namely to abhor whatever the world loves, and
on the other hand, to desire with all his might
whatever the same world shuns. He set our
Lord, despised and made the last of men for our
sake, before his eyes, as his model in humiliation;
and he earnestly desired to be clothed with the
same garments as Christ, to suffer injuries,
mockery, and insult with him. When he fore-
saw that persecution, slander, and other similar
trials were to come upon him in any place, he
remained there with excessive delight. But when
he found people making much of him, he would

---

* I. Corinth. 4, v. 9.   † Jerem. 49, v. 16.
‡ Jerem. 49, v. 15.

protest that he was the worst of sinners, and seek to bring them to a like view of his character. He did this chiefly when, by unanimous consent, he was elected general of his own Society. He ordered several ballots at the election, in order to escape the burden; but the issue being always the same, how could he refuse to comply? Still he put the matter entirely into the hands of his confessor; he made to him a general confession of his whole life so that he might judge him unfit to be general. Finally, in hospitals, among beggars, and the lowest class of men, in his entire way of living he sought with the noblest magnaminity, means to trample on all vain, worldly glory, as well as on himself. *

We, who commend ourselves so much, who are so fretful and impatient when God brings down our pride by some humiliation, disdain to imitate Christ our Lord. He who clings to the world and its laws, seeks honors and fame ; so he who follows Christ despises the empty glory of this world; and if he does not love, he at least ought to bear patiently the injuries, insults and contempt that accompany the livery of Christ. "For I have given you an example, that as I have done to you, so you do also."†

---

* Bull of canonization.   † John, 13, v. 15.

POINT III.—*In heavenly gifts.*—The false goods of this world foster pride; but spiritual goods, that are heavenly gifts, promote humility in the soul that gets them. Hence, in proportion to the number of his heavenly gifts, Ignatius experienced every day humbler sentiments in his soul. Supernatural illuminations of the mind, visions, ecstasies had grown familiar to him; but he turned them all into new means of self abasement. He looked upon himself as a house threatening to fall, and that could not remain upright without supports: hence," the mercy of God," he would say, "holds me up by these means." At other times he viewed himself as a broken stick encased in the gold of divine graces and surrounded by the gifts of God, instead of the fire that he so much deserved. Again, he was a horrid monster, combining so many sins with so many mercies, such utter unworthiness witn such crowds of heavenly favors. Once, when raised from the ground in an ecstasy, and shining with light from heaven, he was heard exclaiming: "O God ! O God of infinite goodness ! how do you still bear with me, so great a sinner ?"* Thus his daily increasing humility constantly fitted him to receive greater spiritual gifts.

---

* Process of canonization.

Do you wonder at your being without any spiritual treasure ; or do you find that God does not listen to your prayers? Blame your pride for all that. God allows us the use of his favors, but he retains the glory of them for himself. You arrogate to yourself that glory which belongs to God alone, and therefore he leaves you bereft of all heavenly goods, and humbles your pride : for, "God resists the proud, but gives his grace to the humble."*

PRAYER.

ST. IGNATIUS! glorious pattern of Christian humility! thou didst know that away in the ages of eternity God was never so glorified as when his Son, for the glory of his Father, "debased himself, taking the form of a servant—being made the reproach of men, and the outcast of the people." ‡ Hence, although adorned so richly with the gifts of heaven, thou didst, in imitation of Jesus Christ, continually humble thyself unsparingly before God and men, and show the greatest ardor for every kind of contempt; so hast thou given the highest glory to God. And I, who by my origin am nothing, who am covered over with the filth of sin, and full of pride, al-

---

* I Pet. 5, v. 5.
† Philippians, 2, v. 7; and Ps. 21, v. 7.

though in utter poverty as regards spiritual gifts, I have always dishonored the majesty of God ! Wherefore, I am as hateful in the eyes of God and of men as thou, O Saint Ignatius, wert dear to them. Holy patron, do not reject my prayer ; teach me true humility ; enable me to see how wretched my soul is, that I may despise and hate myself. I ask all this in order that henceforward I may, by humility, self-contempt, and hatred give as much glory to God as I have hitherto given him offence by my pride. Amen.

MAXIMS.

THE following maxims were delivered by St. Ignatius in an apparition to St. Mary Magdalen of Pazzi :—

1. Interior humility consists in a constant knowledge of our nothingness, and in a love of everything that can bring us to despise ourselves. —This humility is like a ladder with so many rounds that one never gets to the topmost, especially, as by repeated acts the same steps have to be gone up again and again. Hence, as long as soul and body remain together, no one should refrain from the practice of this virtue.

2. Exterior humility shows itself in words, gestures and deeds. We ought to shun, as a blasphemy, any word that does not breathe humility.

Gestures contrary to humility should be avoided with the same care as those opposed to purity. Works that do not conform to humility are to be avoided as a king would avoid dressing his son and heir as a cow boy.

3. To the oil of humility we must add the perfume of holy love. Then consider the glory that acts of humility give to God, the great works that humility performs and the advantages that accrue to the humble soul. Thus humility will be loved, and the soul, with all her might, will seek to acquire it.

EXAMPLE.

THE wonderful humility of St. Ignatius stirred up the wrath of the evil spirit against him. He declared, by the lips of possessed persons, that he had no worse enemy than St. Ignatius; "he has as much humility as I have pride." God exalted his servant for that humility, and gave immense power over evil spirits.* Crowds of people could be cited out of whom the Saint drove the devil. † We shall mention only one among many, that was a triumph of the true faith over heresy. At Ostrog, a town in Poland, a Calvinist woman was possessed. Though knowing only

---

* Roman Breviary. † Raymand, Vol. 9. p. 134.

her mother-tongue, she spoke Latin, German,
and Ruthenian with perfect ease. She related things that she had no natural means of
knowing, described events taking place at great
distances, and gave evidence of extraordinary
strength. The ministers of her religion for a
long time tried, but in vain, to expel the devil
from her. At last, they took her to the Rector of
the Jesuit college at Ostrog, and earnestly begged
of him, to say the prayers of the Church over
her, and free her from her wicked guest. The
Rector promised to do for them whatever he
could ; but first he reproached them for their
errors, and made the devil confess the falsity of
Calvinism. He next ordered a fast of three days,
and on the feast of our Lady's Purification, in
the Church of the Society, which was crowded
with people, having ·repeatedly invoked the
names of the Blessed Virgin Mary and St. Igna
tius, he drove the devil out of the woman,
and forced him to acknowledge that he was
expelled by the power of Mary and Ignatius.
When the poor woman received her conscious-
ness she burst into tears of joy, and renounced
the errors of Calvin, while the by-standers ex-
claimed : "Great is the Lord, and exceedingly
to be praised."* Great is his mother! great is

* Psalm 47, v. 1.

Ignatius! The only true religion is the Catholic religion :—*Marian Annals*, 1627.

PRACTICE.

IN accordance with the teaching of St. Ignatius, "humble thyself in all things, and thou shalt find grace before God."*

EJACULATION.

O GOD! infinitely good God! who still bearest with me who am such a sinner.†

SIXTH MEDITATION.

St. Ignatius a pattern of great, active and productive confidence in God.

POINT I.— *Great confidence.* — St. Ignatius, having renounced the world and given himself wholly to God, placed all his trust in him. It is wonderful what hardships and contempt he had to bear wherever he went. He was ill-treated,

---

* Eccli 3, v. 20.
† S. Ignatius in the process of his Canonization.

thrown into prison, and suffered everything short
of death.*   But equally wonderful, amid all
these crosses and trials, were the serenity of his
soul, his perfect calmness springing from a
heroic reliance on God.   He used to say that he
who forgets himself in order to serve God, has
God for his helper ; and God takes more care of
him than such a man could take of himself.
Wherefore, when slandered and thrown into
prison, he asked no one to defend or protect him.
When about to set out for Jerusalem he made
no provision for the journey, and when, as he
was going along, some friends obliged him to
take some money, he bitterly reproached himself
with want of trust in God, and was on the point
of throwing the money away ; on second thought
however, he gave it all to the poor.   With the
same confidence, when reduced to the greatest
straits and harrassed by men, he undertook many
works of charity.   Living in Rome in times of
great scarcity, and being asked how it was that
while rich people lessened their expenses, he
increased his own, though he had no income to
rely on.   " Don't fear " was his answer, " he who
feeds the birds of the air and clothes the lilies
of the field, will not allow those who work in

---

* Roman Breviary.

the vineyard of the Church for nothing, to want the necessaries of life." Still he did not wish that hope of this kind should encourage sloth. He said: "we should do whatever lay in our power, and that done we were to look upon ourselves as unprofitable servants, and put all our hopes in God."

"Blessed is the man that hath not put his trust in money nor in treasures."* It is good to confide in the Lord rather than to have confidence in man. It is good to trust in the Lord rather than to trust in princes. † They that fear the Lord have hoped in the Lord; he is their helper and their protector. ‡ If you rely on men "lo, thou trusteth upon a broken staff of a reed, upon which if a man lean, it will go into his hand and pierce it." §

POINT II.—*His confidence was active.*—Though the confidence of Ignatius in God was so great, and though he had constantly wonderful proofs of the Divine protection; he still withal considered himself unworthy of being listened to by God. He, therefore, used every means to propitiate the saints and make them his friends and intercessors with God. In matters of importance

---

* Eccli. 31, v. 8.   ‡ Psalm 113, v. 11.
† Psalm 117, v. 8-9.   § Isaiah, 36, v. 6.

he applied now to the saints, at another time to the choirs of angels, to plead his cause before the Queen of heaven.   Again he would pray directly to the Mother of God to urge his cause with her Son. Finally, he would beseech Jesus Christ with tears, not to look upon his sins, but on the merits and intercession of so many of his servants, especially of his own mother, and to move his eternal Father, and all the persons of the ever blessed Trinity to grant his request.   To his prayers he added self-flagellations and long fasts until he obtained what he asked.   And when his prayer was granted, he went the rounds again, returning his thanks with the deepest and humblest gratitude to the saints and angels, to the Blessed Virgin, our Lord and the adorable Trinity.

If, in consequence of our many sins, we do not dare put firm trust in God, let us remember the influence with him of his servants and friends in heaven—what Mary can effect with her Son—the power of Christ with his Father ; let us implore their patronage by constant prayer, and if need be, let us employ bodily penance, and then we shall see the help of the Lord upon us.   What God's justice would refuse to our demerits, his clemency will grant to so many intercessors.   "We have boldness and access with confidence by the faith of him."*

POINT III.—*Rewards of this confidence.*—From his very conversion he reaped, through the influence of the Blessed Virgin particularly, fruits of this confidence in God. He was saved from the many dangers, hardships and persecutions that he met with. In his wants, the angels came several times to his assistance. At one time, our Lord himself, at another, his Blessed Mother appeared to Ignatius, and promised him help and special protection. Among those promises the most celebrated is the one that was given in a church not far from Rome. Ignatius had entered it to pray, and, as was usual with him, he was soon lost in ecstasy. Then the Eternal Father appeared to him surrounded by a bright light, and pointing to our Lord, who appeared also carrying his cross, he praised Ignatius and his companions, and said : "I wish you accept him as your servant." Hereupon our Lord turned to Ignatius, and taking him under his protection, said : "I wish you to serve me. I will help you in Rome." This promise caused Ignatius the sweetest consolation. Addressing his companions, he remarked : "I don't know what is to

---

* Ephes. 3, v. 12.

happen in Rome : but this I do know, that whatever may happen, Jesus Christ will be favorable
to us." He then related to them the foregoing
vision.

O how good is not our God to his servants!
He is so kindly present to them—bestows on
them so much honor and joy—rewards them at
once and increases their joy. Blessed is the man
who relies on the help and fidelity of God alone,
who works out his salvation in filial trust in him
—and who would consider it a sin to entertain a
shadow of doubt with regard to God's sovereign
goodness. "Behold ! God is my Saviour, I will
deal confidently, and will not fear." *

PRAYER.

ADMIRABLE patriarch, St. Ignatius ! I know
now whence came thy unconquerable magnanimity in working and suffering for the greater
glory of God. It arose from thy filial confidence
in God. "For they that hope in the Lord shall
renew their strength—they shall run and not be
weary, they shall walk and not faint."† From
this I also learn why I am so weak, that in the
all important affair of salvation the slightest
difficulty frightens me, and makes me give up

* Isaiah, 12, v. 2.   † Isaiah, 40, v, 31.

living a good life. All this weakness proceeds from my little confidence in God. · The promises of God are, indeed, infallible, and the earth is covered with his mercy: yet my hope in God is not sufficiently strong. The more I rely on my own powers and in the help of men, the more I detract from the confidence that I should place in God alone, the best of Fathers. Lift up my heart, then, O holy patron, that it may fix its refuge in God alone—that it may hope, first for God; secondly, for his kingdom in heaven ; thirdly, for suitable means here on earth to earn that kingdom; and, lastly, that among earthly goods I may seek only those that will help me to obtain eternal posession of God. Amen.

MAXIMS.

1. CONFIDENCE resting on the favor of men, or on riches, is false. True confidence is that which, the greater our penury or our difficulties, the more it leans on God. St. Ignatius supported this saying by the words of the Apostle: "But hope that is seen is not hope. For what a man seeth, why doth he hope for? But if we hope for that which we see not, we wait for it with patience."*

---

* Rom. 8, v. 24-25.

2. There is nothing miraculous in God's help-
ing his servants who hope in him: it would be
a miracle were he to abandon them.   His action
is based on his own promises: "Because he hoped
in me, I will deliver him. . . . I will deliver
him, and I will glorify him." *

3. Serve God with all care and zeal: entrust
all your interests and anxieties to him: " It is
easy for the Lord to save, either by many or by
few."†

Example.

The following fact will bring out more fully the
fatherly providence of God in regard to his servants, and at the same time it will show that the
security and reliance of St. Ignatius were free
from rashness.   When there was no money in
the house to meet the daily expenses, it happened
more than once that a stranger came to the
treasurer and putting into his hands a bag of
gold coin, instantly disappeared without saying a
word.   One evening there was nothing to eat
or drink; nothing to make a fire the next day.
The following morning quite early, a lady sent
a large cart-load of wood to the house. The door-
keeper went to put it in the cellar; but remem-

---

* Psalm 90, v. 14-15.   † I. Kings, 14, v 6.

bering that he had left the house-door open, he hastened back to shut it. What was his surprise to find in the hall some bushels of wheat and barrels of wine. No one could ever find out who sent these presents. By deeds like these, which often happened, God provided for the wants of his servants.—*Bollandists for July.*

PRACTICE.

MAKE acts of hope in God with all your heart.

EJACULATION.

"IN thee, O Lord, have I hoped ; let me never be confounded."*

---

* Psalm 30, v. 1.

SEVENTH MEDITATION.

The Unitive Way.

St. Ignatius, a pattern of most ardent love for God, by his spiritual enlightenment, by his earnestness and the elevation of his thoughts.

Point I.—*His spiritual enlightenment.*—Charity is a heavenly fire that illumines the mind, inflames the heart, and lifts the entire soul up to God. The vast light which love for God converged upon the mind of Ignatius, is manifest from the teaching scattered up and down his Exercises with regard to meditation, to the discerning of the actions of the various spirits, what paths are safe, and what unsafe in the spiritual life. St. Philip Neri considered him a master in the art of directing souls, and in the science of the Saints; for he often saw the countenance of Ignatius radiant with heavenly light, and thence conjectured the fulness of light that possessed his soul. Nor was this excellence of St. Ignatius astonishing. God disengaged him from the senses and showed him by himself, by the angels, the saints, the Blessed Virgin, or even our Lord himself— who were all, so to say, on familiar terms with Ignatius—the power of the Creator, the infinite wisdom of the redemption, the order and purpose of creatures, the efficacy of the sacraments, the marvellous workings of divine grace in a soul, and many other wonders of the same kind.

The wise ones of the world who style themselves enlightened, but who measure withal everything divine by the senses and human passions, deserve rather to be called foolish and blind. "The sensual man perceiveth not the things that are of the spirit of God." * The Holy Ghost looks for a heart free from all the defilements of the flesh, and a mind cleaving to God with a lively faith, before he communicates by charity those teachings, that heavenly learning, which outstrip our natural powers. "Blessed are the clean of heart, for they shall see God." †

Point II.—*His earnestness.*—The charity of God was poured out in the heart of Ignatius by the Holy Ghost, who was given to him. ‡ As in the case of the Apostles, a tongue of fire appeared, and rested upon him, and he was filled with the Holy Ghost. § Hence, frequently during day and night, amid sighs and tears, he opened his heart to God, particularly to our Lord on the cross, or hidden in the Blessed Eucharist ; and

---

* I Corinth., 2, v. 14.
† Matt., 5, v. 8.
‡ Rom., 5, v. 5.
§ Acts, 2, v. 3.

breaking forth into his usual exclamation, asking
still greater love for God, he would say: "Lord,
let me love thee, and for no other purpose than
to love thee more." On occasions of this kind,
his affections grew so warm that he fainted, as it
were, and the only signs of life that he gave, were
a flushed countenance and violent beating of his
heart. It cannot be wonderful, therefore, that
no matter how pressed by business, as soon as he
invoked God, or heard the name of Jesus, his
face was lit up, his heart burned, he overflowed
with joy, and he dropped to rest in the embrace
of God, or of Christ. He once made, with great
candor, the wonderful declaration, that he could
not live by the sole powers of nature. Indeed it
was a common impression among those who saw
more closely the fires of divine love, amid which
he spent his days, that he lived his transfigured
life far more on divine charity than on natural
strength. "I live, now not I; but Christ liveth
in me." *

"Thou shalt love the Lord thy God, with thy
whole heart, and with thy whole soul, and with
thy whole mind,"† says Jesus Christ. We do this
when, in comparison with him, we make no
account of all else; when, as St. Ignatius taught,

---

* Galatians, 2, v. 20.   † Matt. 22, v. 37.

we so employ the faculties of our soul in loving
God, that our memory recalls his love for us, and
his benefits to us; our mind reflects carefully on the
Divine perfections; our will loves those perfections—delights in them—desires eagerly to please
God, to do and suffer all things out of love for
God. Be ashamed of yourself in case your heart
is still far from such love for God. "Look, and
make it according to the pattern that was shown
thee"* in Ignatius. The above-mentioned exercise of your memory, understanding and will,
will kindle the fire of charity in your heart. "In
my meditation a fire shall flame out." †

POINT III.—*Elevation of his thoughts.*—The
charity in which his soul abounded, so lifted Ignatius up to God, that he was able to say with
St. Paul: "Our conversation is in heaven." ‡
Often while meditating on heavenly things, or
amid the sublime emotions of the Canonical
hours, his soul rushed to God with such vehe-
mence, that his body was all surrounded with
light, and raised from the ground. He would see
heaven open before him, gaze on its shining
crowds of citizens, and distinguish their pecu-
liar glory. Our Lord frequently showed himself
to the Saint in the Blessed Eucharist, and ex-
plained to him the ineffable manner in which he

---

* Exodus, 25, v. 40.　　　† Psalm 38, v. 4.
‡ Philippians, 3, v. 20.

at one and the same time dwells under the sacred
species and reigns gloriously in heaven. There
is a little book containing his visions and spiritual
illuminations, which he received at mass, during
a space of four months, while he was drawing up
the constitutions of his Society. He used to put
these favors in a sort of diary so as to foster piety
and keep a remembrance of them. Before his
death, however, he took care to destroy all writings
of the kind; a few leaves escaped his search, and
they form the little book in question. In it he
tells us, that he saw our Lord mediating for him
with the Father, the Blessed Virgin most lovingly
presenting him, her client, to her Son, and ap-
proving the Constitutions that he had framed.
Meanwhile, he, himself, was fired with divine
love, but so illuminating and sweet that he felt
himself most closely united to divine love, received incredible light from it, and heard voices
and harmonies beautiful beyond all earthly ex-
pression.   "At times," the Saint writes, "so high
was I raised, such was the spiritual light vouch-
safed to me about God, his unity, the Trinity,
that there seemed to be nothing more for me to
learn. I knew, I felt, I saw. My knowledge
was so surprising, that I incessantly cried out
in admiration: What am I? What do I merit?
How has this light come to me?" These, and

many other wonders, are spoken of in the afore-
mentioned book, and more at length, in the au-
thentic inquiry made about Ignatius at Toledo.*
There is a shorter account of all these matters in
an illustrated work on the life of the Saint. Here
is one of its titles: " He writes the Constitutions of
the Society of Jesus, and has, while doing so,
many visions of the Adorable Trinity, who bestow much light on him, and of the Blessed
Virgin, who gives her approbation to what he was
writing."

Blessed soul ! so wonderfully one with God—
and happy in him, as far as one can be in this
world.—" God is not far from every one of us : for
in him we live, and move, and be." † But our
soul, involved in earthly affections, "has forgotten
God, her Saviour, and has not remembered her
strong helper." ‡ Let us awake, then, and rise
out of the mire of our sins. Let us not love the
world nor the things that are in the world. §
Let us therefore love God, because God first hath
loved us. ‖

---

* See works of the Ven. Father Lancicius. Vol. 2,
opusc. 17.

† Acts, 17, v. 27-28.   § I John, 2, v. 15.
‡ Isaiah, 17, v. 10.   ‖ I John, 4, v. 19.

PRAYER.

THY Seraphic love for God, O holy Ignatius, condemns and puts to confusion my negligence and lukewarmness in loving him. My heart is so depraved that it loves earthly goods, and even my vices and sins; and has no care to love the God, whom it was created to love. Thy heart, whilst thou wert in this world, burned with a constant desire to enkindle in every one a great love for God. Now that thou art in heaven this desire must be far greater. I therefore offer thee my heart, that thou mayest cleanse it from all disorderly affections, fire it every day more and more with thy love, and teach it to love God the Sovereign good. Whilst, in order to obtain this grace, I use the words with which thou wert wont to dedicate thyself wholly to God, ask for me, I beg of thee, the favor of consecrating myself to God forevermore with all thy fervor.

MAXIMS.

1. IF the blessed in heaven could grieve, they would go into mourning as a sign of sorrow and wailing for those who were once fervent in the service of God, but afterwards fell into lukewarmness. If you have grown languid in love

for God, you have grieved Jerusalem that nursed you. *

2. We should watch constantly over the purity of our hearts, and by frequent aspirations raise them to God who is everywhere present : for charity does not spring up in an unclean, but in a clean heart. †

3. We should often visit the Blessed Sacrament, which is the guarantee and feeder of love. The time immediately after holy Communion is most valuable ; and should be entirely given to God and to divine love ; for then God dwells in us, and we in him. "He that eateth my flesh abideth in me, and I in him." ‡

EXAMPLE.

God rewarded the love of St. Ignatius not only by conferring on him the essential happiness of heaven, which is man's chief blessedness ; but he also granted him very great glory here on earth. He had not yet reached the honors of canonization when in Catalayud, a town of Aragon, in Spain, an angel appeared to a pious Canon, who delighted in having in his house fine paintings of the founders of the various religious orders.

---

* Baruch, 4, v. 8.   † I Timothy, I, v. 5.
‡ John, 6, v. 57.

The angel presented himself as a stranger on his travels   Seeing that the portrait of Ignatius was not in the Canon's collection, he offered to paint it.   His offer was accepted and he set to work. A short while after he was summoned to dinner ; but he refused to go, saying that his work was going on well and he did not wish to leave it. At the end of dinner the painter was again called, and looked for everywhere ; but he could not be found.   He had disappeared, leaving a portrait of St. Ignatius surrounded by rays of light, and surpassing in beauty all the others possessed by the Canon.   This painting was afterwards sent to Munebrega, and was there very much honored by crowds of people.   Many and great favors were obtained by those who prayed before it to St. Ignatius.   Within the space of a month more than a hundred miracles were wrought at Mune-brega ; among them was the restoration to life of a boy and a little girl, who had died sometime previously.—*Alphonsus Andrada, History of the Picture of Munebrega, Madrid, 1669.*

PRACTICE.

WITH frequent acts of charity thou wilt love the Lord, thy God, with thy whole heart.*

---

* Mathew, xxvii, v. 57.

EJACULATION.

LORD grant me to love thee, and for no other object but to love thee more and more.—*St. Ignatius.*

EIGHTH MEDITATION.

St. Ignatius a pattern of zeal for souls in his desires, his labors, and in the works he set on foot for this purpose.

POINT I.—*His desires.*—Zeal for souls is an effect of charity, which makes one love God and bring others to love him. The greater our love for God, the greater will be our zeal. From the beginning of his conversion, love for God burned so ardently in his soul, that even in the night-time he was found raised from the ground shining with light, and exclaiming amid sighs and tears ; "O my God ! O my Lord ! If men only know thee, they would never sin." At other times,

raised from the ground in a kneeling posture, his
eyes dazzling with light, and his face uplifted towards heaven, he would say : "Dearest Jesus ! if
men only loved thee." And as the bitter death
that the Son of God underwent for the salvation
of men, was always present to the mind of Ignatius, he used often to exclaim :   "Would it were
in my power to die a thousand times a day, even
in the worst torments, for Christ and for the salvation of one soul." No wonder then that when
he was General of his Society, he led through
the streets a crowd of abandoned women whom
he had reclaimed, to a house where their virtue
would be out of danger. Whilst he was engaged
in this work some one remarked to him that he
was losing his time, because such women easily
fall back into their sins ; Ignatius answered
that he would consider himself amply rewarded
by merely preventing the sins that any one of
these poor creatures would commit in a night.
How wonderful, too, is not that assertion of the
Saint which the Tribunal of the Rota has so ex-
tolled, and which he made with so much earnestness, viz : Were the choice given to me, I would
·rather serve God here and save souls, in uncertainty of eternal happiness, than die at this
moment in the full assurance of going to heaven.
If St. Ignatius preferred the salvation of others

to his own certain and immediate happiness for eternity, can we hesitate for our own eternal salvation to renounce our evil desires and concupiscences, and to remove all obstacles to our neighbors' salvation ? The chief object for which we have to strive, is eternity. For " all gold in comparison of it, is as a little sand, and silver in respect to her shall be counted as clay."*

POINT II.—*His labors.*—The labors of St. Ignatius were not behind his vehement desires for saving souls. From the first days of his conversion he resolved to avoid no danger, to shrink from no toil in trying to bring souls to God, and to devote himself unceasingly, as long as his life would last, to this most important work. He kept his resolution wherever he lived. Hence, when the process for his canonization began, so many notable conversions of great sinners, abandoned women, Jews and heretics, were related that every city in which Ignatius spent any time, looked upon him as its apostle. Out of that first resolve came that devotedness, which the Holy Church calls remarkable, which led Ignatius, at the age of three and thirty, for the purpose of being more useful to souls, to study grammar first, and afterwards philosophy and theology.

---

* Wisdom, 7, v. 9.

Later on, he went over these studies again in
Paris, living, meanwhile, on alms, omitting none
of his practices of charity, humility and mortification, and having to bear ridicule, blows, and
imprisonment, during his labors for souls.   How
often, too, did not the devil, as it were, foreseeing
the future, try to interrupt his studies !   When,
in the learning of the Latin grammar, he met
the verb *to love*, or any other word of the kind,
the enemy would direct his thoughts to God; at
other times, he would fill his mind with light,
and lay bare to him the hidden sense of Holy
Scripture.   And all this was done in order to
draw off the mind of Ignatius from his books.
But the attempt did not succeed; it merely gave
Ignatius a new occasion to triumph gloriously
over himself.   For, as soon as he saw the wiles of
the evil one, he cast himself at the feet of his
master, begging him in earnest to exact from him
every day, the same task as from the other stu-
dents, and to be punished like them, in word or
deed, when found guilty of any negligence in
the performance of duty.   If St. Ignatius toiled
so ardently for the salvation of others, we can
imagine what we ought to undertake for our own
souls.   In case we do not do much for them, it
is not our want of power, but of will we have to
blame.   For grace is always at our door, and at

every moment we can gain new help through prayer. Well, then, in order that God may not have to condemn our error on Judgment Day, when it will be to late to correct it, let us now, at this very time, " labor the more, that by good works we may make sure our calling and election." *

POINT III.—*The works he established.*—St. Ignatius "not willing that any should perish, but that all should return to penance," † instituted a religious order that should help to oppose idolatry, Judaism, and heresy. That order was also to restore piety among Catholics, to teach catechism, to give retreats and missions, and to promote the frequent reception of the Sacraments. To the three vows of poverty, chastity and obedience, usual in all religious orders, it adds a fourth, whereby it binds itself to go on any mission, entrusted to it by the Holy See, without asking any pecuniary means for the journey. All these are works belonging to the Institute of Ignatius. In conformity with this method of life, he sent St. Francis Xavier to preach the Gospel in India, and others for a similar purpose into various parts of the world. At the same time, he opened houses of education everywhere for the literary

---

* II Peter, I, v. 10.   † II Peter, 3, v. 9.

and Christian formation of youth. He founded
the German College in Rome, and established
refuges for fallen women, or poor girls in danger,
and orphanages for children of both sexes. Indeed, there was no end to the pious works that
his untiring zeal for souls made him undertake,
and carry on until the day of his death.* Truly,
as Pope Gregory XV. said, Ignatius was a man
very great for saving the elect of God. † He
was a new apostle, as the Rota styled him. He
had a soul larger than the world; he went
through labors, founded institutions, reaped fruits,
worthy of any apostle.

"God gave commandment to everyone con-
cerning his neighbor." ‡ Therefore, everyone
should help his neighbor by the example of good
works, by timely advice, by assiduous prayer to
God. What of those, who, on the contrary, by
their bad lives, wicked example, scandalous
talk, far from gaining souls to Christ, lead them
to perdition? Says our Lord: "Wo, to that man
by whom the scandal cometh." §

PRAYER.

SINCE thou, most holy patriarch, with so much
ardor, with such labors, and by so many insti-

---

tutions, didst seek to save all men, hear, I beseech thee, the prayers which I suppliantly address thee, in accordance with the wishes of thine own heart. Lo I "I have gone astray, like a sheep that is lost."* Seek thy wretched little client, who is covered with the filth of many sins, constantly harassed by the seductions of the world, the snares of the devil, and in danger of eternal damnation. Stretch out thy hands to me in my poverty, † that I may rise out of the slough of sin, and enter the path of salvation. Indeed "I know my sin, and my iniquity is always before me." ‡ I am sorry that I so often offended my God, who is the Sovereign good. Obtain for me, holy patron, that this sorrow may go on increasing until my death, and that through thee, I may derive mercy from God. "Let thy hand be with me to save me." "Help me and I shall be saved.‖ Amen.

MAXIMS.

1. WERE God to cast me into hell without any fault of mine, my greatest pain would be, not the tortures of the place, but to listen to the blasphemies which are there uttered against God.

---

* Psalm, 1:8, v. 176.   † Psalm, 50, v. 5.
† Eccli. 7, v. 36.   ‖ Psalm 118, v. 173, 117.

Learn from St. Ignatius to abhor openly all offences against God, saying sincerely with him: "I have hated and abhorred inquity." *

2. In order that talents and other natural gifts may do good, they must be governed by the interior spirit, and draw from it all their force and efficacy. For we are instruments of the Lord: "In his hand are both we and our words, and all wisdom, and the knowledge and skill of works." †

3. To gain souls to God, a circle of mutual influence is required; namely, prayer mounting up to God, and obtaining grace from him; and patient action, descending to our neighbor. All the art of gaining souls to God lies in this: "I have labored in my groanings." ‡

EXAMPLE.

As formerly on earth, so now in glory, St. Ignatius procures heavenly remedies for diseased souls more readily than for diseased bodies. In the year 1602, there was, at Gandia, in Spain, a woman who led an immoral life with a young man. At last, she began to desire to rise out of her wretched state, but her bad habits made fearful opposition to her holy purpose. In her distress she implored the help of Ignatius.

---

* Psalm 118, v. 163.   † Wisdom, 7, v. 16.
‡ Psalm 6, v. 7.

Scarcely had she hung the Saint's portrait over
her bed, when she felt such disgust for the man
she had hitherto loved so madly, that she could
not even bear the sight of him.—*Bollandists for
July.*

PRACTICE.

THROUGH the example of good works, "let your
light so shine before men, that they may see your
good works, and glorify your Father, who is in
heaven.*"

EJACULATION.

ST. IGNATIUS, let thy hand be with me to save
me; help me, and I shall be saved.†

---

* Matthew, 5, v. 16.   † Psalm 118, v. 173, 117

NINTH MEDITATION.

The heart of St. Ignatius was a pattern of interior life towards God, towards himself, and towards his neighbor.

POINT I.—*Towards God.*—He who wants to serve God must be an interior man—that is to say, he must work far more with the interior affections of his heart than by external action. St. Ignatius taught this doctrine, and with sovereign perfection he directed his heart in accordance with it in regard to God, to himself and his neighbor. And first with respect to God. For from the date of his conversion, he made this a law for himself which he never afterwards transgressed—namely, that thenceforward he would seek only God and his greater glory. Wherefore it never entered into his mind to offer to God, as an expiation for his sins, a single one of the rigid austerities which he then began to practice: for he feared lest his own interests should detract even one tittle from that greater glory. Every hour indeed he looked into all his actions; nor was he satisfied with merely avoiding faults and performing some virtuous deeds during that time. He also inquired, whether he could not have served God better; nay, more, when he had

several things to do, he always gave the prefer-
ence to what he thought would be more glorious
to God. The Rota compresses all this into the
following words: He burned with such love for
God, that he sought for him all day. He thought
of nothing else—desired nothing else—than to
please God, and do his adorable will. He
therefore put himself entirely in God's hands, and
determined to seek him even at the expense of
everything. All his thoughts, all his word sand
works were referred to God as to their end; they
were for God, for His honor and glory alone.
The saying: *for the greater glory of God*, was a
watchword that was constantly on his lips.

"God created all nations to his own praise, and
name and glory."* In order, therefore, to cor-
respond fully with the end for which he is
made, every one should direct all his actions,
words and thoughts to God and to his greater
glory. Those who do not work for that end,
"their hope is vain, and their labors withou,
fruit, and their works unprofitable."† Therefore,
"whether you eat or drink, or whatsoever else you
do, do all to the glory of God."‡

Point II.—*Towards himself.*—"The greatest ob

---

* Deuteron, 26, v. 19.   † Wisdom, 3, v. 11.
‡ I Cor. 10, v. 31.

stacle to the rising of our heart to God, is self-love," said St. Ignatius, and therefore he reduced the whole art of spiritual progress to this one principle: *Conquer thyself.* Hence, his chief aim was to restrain the emotions of the soul, and to overcome every natural repugnance. By nature he was of a bilious and ardent disposition; yet by constant self-resistance he became altogether another man. Even physicians supposed that he was of a cold, phlegmatic character, and consequently made sad mistakes in their treatment. This wonderful self-discipline gave him entire command, as the Rota said, over all the movements of his soul and body, and made them dutiful servants of virtue and of God's greater glory. But let us learn from the Saint himself the foundations which he laid in his heart in order to raise this temple of peace to the greater glory of God. "It belongs to God," he used to say, "to dispose of us. Whether he takes anything from us or hurts us, or whether he gives us something and caresses us, he is equally holy and good. In both cases we should equally love and praise that goodness and holiness. Moreover, as all things are to be loved and feared in so far as God bids us love or fear them, our heart has to direct its loves and fears, according to this rule, without ever overstepping it, espe-

cially as God shows such condescension as to be
honored and glorified by the little services which
we, his lowly creatures, render him."—Would that
we established this law in our hearts : Would
that we were always so disposed and so resigned
towards God, whether he sends us good or evil,
as to seek only his glory, to please him and to
do his will. But if, contrary to his command, we
seek ourselves and satisfy our rebellious desires,
we can never be at peace with him, nor with our
own conscience. "There is no peace to the
wicked, saith the Lord."*

POINT III.—*Towards his neighbor.*—St. Ignatius spared no pains to win the good will of men
in order to gain them over to Christ. He began
by studying the dispositions and character of
people with whom he had to deal, and then in
so far as it was allowable, he caught each one
with his own bait, as the saying goes. He
would put up with their harshness and arrog-
ance, accomodate himself to their silliness and
folly, bear with and overlook their rudeness and
insulting behavior, and yield to them in all
things as far as virtue would permit. When in
this way he had gained them over to himself, he
set to work upon them, and with slow and cau-

* Isaiah, 48, v. 22.

tious management he gradually brought them to a sense of duty and the practice of religion. This holy artifice and the bright example of his own sanctity reclaimed many from heresy to the Catholic faith, or from a sinful to a good life, and induced many also to despise everything earthly and embrace the salutary counsels of Christ. But his charity chiefly displayed itself where he found the fuller image of Christ, namely, among the poor and his own children, who had given themselves up to his care and direction. He was so devoted to the poor and the sick, to orphans and catechumens, to unfortunate women, to girls in danger of losing their virtue, and similar classes of persons, that everyone among them looked up to him as to a most affectionate parent. Towards his own children such was his charity that he considered their temptations and sufferings his own; and hence, he did everything to console, direct, encourage and inflame them with love for God. Nor in doing so did he content himself with words alone ; he prayed and fasted for them, and chastised his body in many ways so as to obtain the necessary graces for them. Hence, everyone thought himself the child of his tears and sorrows. In this manner, unto the greater glory of God, Ignatius was made all to all, that he might save all.*

"This Commandment we have from God, that he who loveth God, love also his brother."* "Therefore from love for God charity is patient, kind, seeketh not her own, is not provoked to anger, thinketh no evil, beareth all things. "† It tries to close hell and open heaven to all, in order that the number of those loving God and his greater glory should increase forever. Wherefore "to love one's neighbor as one's self is a greater thing than all holocausts and sacrifices. ‡

PRAYER.

IN thy heart, O blessed Ignatius, that was so upright with God, so severe towards thyself, so overflowing with love for its neighbor, and always so intent on the greater service of God, I see, as in a mirror, the wickedness of my own heart, and I am covered with shame at the sight. God created my heart and loaded it with spiritual gifts for his own glory; and I have used that heart's affections and God's favors to offend him. While seeking myself and indulging my evil desires, I am troubled in mind, drawn here and there ; my conscience loudly upbraids me ; I am not myself any more. Being, then, almost unable

---

* John, 4, v. 21.　　　† Corinth. 13, v. 4-7.
‡ Mark, 12, v. 33.

to bear myself, how can I sympathise with my
neighbor, or patiently bear his defects.   Here,   .
O holy patron, is a faithful description of my
heart.   How different it is from thy heart.   I lay
it before thee that thou mayest take pity on it.
Depraved as it is, I offer it to thee that thou
mayest renew a right spirit within it.   So, that
like thee, it may seek only God and his glory—
that henceforward I may be at peace with God,
with myself and my neighbor, until through
thee I become a sharer forever in the glory of
God in heaven.   Amen.

Maxims.

1. For him who works with all possible dili-
gence a precious crown is laid up' in heaven.
This crown is proportioned, not so much to the
good works we do, as to the fervor with which
we do them.   God makes more account of our
dispositions than of our deeds.   Therefore thou
shalt follow justly after that which is just.*

2. He who has a stubborn and fiery nature
should not lose courage in case he seeks to conquer that nature.   Rather let him be assured
that one victory gained over himself, will be of
greater value before God than many victories

---

* Dueteron. 16, v. 20.

over an easy and peaceful nature. God has
given such a man a strong conflict that he may
overcome.*

3. In our dealings with men we ought to imitate the angels. Though they dwell on earth for
our protection, still they never cease to love God.
Our conversation should always be in heaven.†

EXAMPLE.

It was not only while living in this world that
St. Ignatius showed the most ardent charity for
his spiritual children. He has done the same
since he went to reign with the blessed in heaven.
There dwelt in Barcelona a widow named Agnes
Pascual, with her son John, a young man of
eighteen. They assisted Ignatius in his need,
and had reaped much spiritual profit from his
direction and intercourse. When he left Barcelona for Paris, they, out of affection, accompanied him some miles. As they were about to
part, Ignatius embraced John, and gave him
some advice for the remainder of his life. But
the young man said: "You have done so much
for others that they have embraced a life of perfection, or have at least made great progress in
virtue. Why do you leave me so unfinished

---

* Wisdom, 10, v. 12.　　†Philip., 3, v. 20.

and imperfect? What will become of me in
your absence? If you allow me, I shall follow
you wherever you go." "Take courage," replied
Ignatius, "you will not want occasions for suffering and for working for God. When older
you will marry, and meet with many crosses that
will not allow you to give way to pleasure, or
neglect imploring the Divine assistance. But all
these trials will end in the salvation of your
soul." Events justified the prediction. Some
years after John married, and had a large family.
He was not rich. He lent nearly all the money
he owned; his creditors cheated him, and left
him penniless. At this time Ignatius lived in
Rome, yet he saw everything that happened to
John. He wrote to him to console him, and
make him resign himself fully to God's holy will.
One day John rose before the dawn and went to
church. Ignatius was now dead, and John
prayed to him: "Holy father, who art now in
heaven, thou seest the sorrow and affliction that
have come upon me in accordance with thy
prediction. I need patience. I beg thee to
ask it of God for me—and also that according
to thy promise, everything may end well for me,
and that I may save my soul." While John was
praying thus he shed many tears. Suddenly
the entire church was brilliantly lit up. John

heard delightful music, and saw a great crowd of angels and saints in it. Among them was a man of venerable mien, dressed as a priest about to celebrate, who having adored the Blessed Sacrament at St. Eulalia's altar, was incensing it with sweet smelling incense. Having done this, as he was about to go away, he approached John, who was in rapture at the whole vision and overflowing with joy. Recognizing St. Ignatius, John threw himself at his feet. The Saint looked at him smilingly, and said: do you remember me? I have not forgotten you. Have courage; everything will turn out well for you, as I told you. He then gave John his blessing, and vanished. Immediately John began to exclaim: O Father! O holy Father Ignatius! Some priests, who were near, hearing these words ran to John, and asked him what was the matter. Weeping and sobbing, John told them all that had happened. Ever afterwards, the bare remembrance of the looks, words and promise of Ignatius on this occasion gave John the greatest relief and consolation in all his trials.—*Bartoli, Book I., n.* 31.

PRACTICE.

FOR the greater glory of God overcome yourself in all things.

EJACULATION.

"NOT to us, O Lord, not to us, but to thy name give glory."[*]

TENTH MEDITATION.

The death of St. Ignatius was precious—in his desire for it—in the sentiments attending it—in the glory that followed it.

POINT I.—*His desires.*—The more God shed the light of his countenance upon Ignatius, whether by interior illuminations or by visions in which even our Lord himself treated him with sovereign affection, the stronger grew his desire to see God as he is in himself, to be with Christ and be released from the shackles of the body. For this reason it was his habit to look up at the starry firmament, to run over in his mind the joys of heaven, to express his desires to the king

---

[*] Ps. 113, v. 1.

of glory—to sigh and weep in order to show God
how eager he was, how ardently he longed for
him. He begged God to take compassion on
him and soon dismiss him in peace. Then cast-
ing his eyes on earth, he would be filled with
contempt for it and cry out : "How vile the
earth seems to me when I look up at the
heavens!" When he heard anyone express a
wish to live long, or saw persons taking means
lest death should overtake them before the end
of this or that work, he would say : "How can
we deceive ourselves with the hope of a long life,
and rob ourselves of the joy of a speedy death,
which God seeks to foster in us by hiding from
us the time at which we shall die." Whenever
he became seriously ill, he would immediately
suppose that he was about to die, and that
thought would throw him into ecstasies, to the
great danger of his health. In those circum-
stances physicians used to forbid him to think
on heavenly subjects. Yet in all these burning
desires it was not an end of his labors, or entrance into eternal joys that he had in view ; for
he was so free from self-seeking that he was often
heard to declare that he could not live if he saw
anything not wholly divine in his heart. Wherefore with the sincerest and purest love he looked
solely to God and his glory : for from his ex-

traordinary insight into the divine goodness, he knew that he could love and exalt his God with far greater perfection in heaven than on earth.

We, poor exiles in this vale of tears, if we love God with our whole heart, should imitate the holy desires of Ignatius, and often exclaim with the apostle: "Unhappy man that I am, who shall deliver me from the body of this death?" * ": I have a desire to be dissolved and to be with Christ. †" Or with David: "Wo is me, that my sojourning is prolonged. My soul hath been long·a sojourner." ‡ "When shall I come and appear before the face of God?" § Such desires are very effective in withdrawing souls from earthly affections and in imbuing them with heavenly dispositions. "And every one that hath this hope in him sanctifieth himself, as he also is holy."‖

Point II.—*The dispositions that accompanied it.*— To fully satisfy the desires of Ignatius, God made known to him the hour of his death, and that he would die as he had asked to do, namely, when no one would expect it, so that visits of condolence, and so forth, might not prevent him from using all his time in preparing his soul. He

---

* Rom. 7, v. 24.   ‡ Ps. 119, v. 5-6.
† Philip, 1, v. 23.   § Ps. 41, v. 3.
‖ I. John, 8, v. 3.

therefore arranged everything that concerned his order, and wrote to some friends at a distance to inform them of his approaching departure. After that he went into retirement and gave himself up to contemplation. During this holy exercise a deadly fever came over him. Yet, though inwardly he was all on fire, there was nothing apparent that could indicate an early death. He seemed, indeed, weak and weary, but these symptoms, caused no anxiety to those he lived with, him, or to his physicians. However, Ignatius knew well that the Lord was coming. He received holy communion, and secretly sent a messenger to ask the Holy Father's blessing and an indulgence. He then spent the last night of his life in sweet communing with God, to whom he was hastening with all the energy of his heart. Relying on what the physicians had said, the people of the house were without apprehension, and they ascribed his talking, sighing and tears, to some of his accustomed visions. Thus matters went on until up to the last hour of his life. Then our Lord and his Virgin Mother, with crowds of angels came to receive his soul, and take it with them to heaven. Directly he fixed his eyes on his Redeemer and the Blessed Virgin, joined his hands, put on a look of wonderful serenity, repeated the holy names of

Jesus and Mary, and fled from earth to rest in
the Lord.   " Precious in the sight of the Lord is
the death of his saints."*

Everyone is anxious for the death of the just;
few, however, prepare themselves for such a
death.   Let filial fear and the love of God keep
us now from sin.   Let us do now, diligently,
what at the hour of death we shall wish to have
done.   Let us now familiarize ourselves with acts
of faith, hope, charity; desire to see God, and
resignation to his holy will ; so that habit may
enable us to elicit them with great fervor when
we are about to die.   " We shall reap what we
sow."†

POINT III.—*Glory that followed his death.*—
" Whosoever shall glorify me, him will I glorify,"‡
says the Lord.   The glory, then, to which St.
Ignatius is raised in heaven, is measured by the
zeal which he always showed for glorifying God
most perfectly in himself and in all mankind.
We need not wonder, then, at the saying of one
who witnessed the entrance of Ignatius into
heaven,—namely, that he was brighter than the
sun, and no triumph could surpass his.   One
of the sons of Ignatius being at the point of

* Ps. 115, v. 15.   † Galatians, 6, v. 8.
‡ I. Kings, 2, v. 30.

death, was invited by his blessed father to follow
him to heaven. While the patient was describing
the splendor of his father's entrance into the
house of the Lord, suddenly he was seized with
such joy that he expired, and went to join him.

But to portray more clearly the glory of the
Saint with God, we must relate the vision of St.
Mary Magdalen, of Pazzi. It took place on De-
cember 26, 1559, and was given to her in order
that she might see how high St. Ignatius is in
heaven. First, she beheld the glory of St. John,
Apostle and Evangelist. She saw that God
took so much delight in his soul that there
seemed to be no one else in heaven. Next, she
was shown the glory of Ignatius, and she learned
that God was as well pleased with him as with
St. John. Whilst she was looking on and ad-
miring the equal glory of the two Saints, God
said to her : "The spirit of John and of Ignatius
was all one. The scope of each of them in all
his actions was love for God and for his neighbor. It was with bonds of charity that they
drew souls to God." St. Mary Magdalen, then,
understood from God that his complacency in
the soul of Ignatius was renewed and increased
every time a soul is brought to him through the
direction and spiritual doctrine that the Saint has
left behind him on earth. Hence, in this same

ecstasy the Saint was heard exclaiming : "Of all who live on earth there is no one whose spirit is like unto that of Ignatius. For by the exercise of interior acts he leads souls to salvation and perfection, and teaches how pleasing such works are to God. Thence springs a love which renders hard and bitter things sweet and easy, and makes them be undertaken with the greatest readiness."* If in heaven Ignatius enjoys the same glory as the beloved disciple, because both loved equally on earth, and thereby glorified God in themselves and in others, do you, also, all your actions out of a similar spirit for God and for your neighbor. Glorify God in this way that now and forever he may be well pleased with you, and after this exile crown you with honor and glory for all eternity. " Love is the keeping of laws, and the keeping of laws is the firm foundation of incorruption."†

PRAYER.

To beg the protection of St. Ignatius at the hour of death.

How precious, O holy patriarch, was not thy death in the sight of God. I congratulate thee,

---

* Revelation of St Mary Magdalen, of Pazzi.
† Wisdom, 6, v. 19.

and I return the warmest thanks to thee, O holy
Redeemer, and to thy Virgin Mother, who most
lovingly were present with Ignatius when he was
dying. What kind of a death shall I die? When
I shall be about to die, "the devil will come
down unto me, having great wrath, knowing that
he hath but a short time," * then truly I shall
be in need of most powerful protection. I implore thy aid, holy patron. As a reward of thy
most ardent zeal for the safety of souls, which
mainly depends on the last moments of life,
God has granted thee special power to protect
thy clients at the moment of death, and allowed
thee often to encourage the dying by thy visible
presence. Therefore, I pray and beseech thee,
not to abandon me at that hour, nor to allow my
soul to go forth from the body burdened with
mortal sin. Grant that now, while I have time,
I may in the spirit of charity, glorify God by all
my works, and thus prepare myself for the final
combat, and merit to enter, after death, into joy
without end. Amen.

MAXIMS.

1. WERE you now about to die, what mode of
life would you wish to have chosen — how would

---

* Apocal., 12, v. 12.

you like to have done each of your actions? Act in that way, and resolve always to do so. In his Spiritual Exercises, St. Ignatius lays down this maxim as a means to repel all the suggestions of the devil, the world and our own passions : "O death, thy sentence is good."[*]

2. The devil, who is the father of lying, readily holds out to you a long life so that you may neglect the present. But if we are certain of the present, we are entirely in the dark as to the future. How foolish then to overlook a present certainty for a future uncertainty. "I know not how long I shall continue, and whether after a-while my Maker may take me away."[†] To stir ourselves up to do good we should often repeat the words with energy : Therefore while we have time let us work good,[‡] and so work it as if we should die after each action ; that is to say, with such an intention and fervor that no particle of its good may be lost to us. "Blessed is that servant whom when his Lord shall come, he shall find so doing."[§]

3. There is another trick of the devil against which we must guard with no less care. When that deceiver sees a man serving God faithfully

---

* Eccli. 41, v. 3.   ‡ Galatians, 6, v. 10.
† Job, 33, v. 22.   § Matt. 24, v. 46.

in a state of perfection, he tries to turn him away from perfection, and bring him, little by little, down to an easier kind of life. For this purpose he holds up to his mind a form of life quite in keeping with virtue, yet very different from the state the man is now in. The devil clothes this kind of life in colors so glowing and attractive that a person not on his guard falls into the snare, and carried away by a semblance of good, gives up his own excellent state of life to follow that new one. Again, in order to prevent us from doing the good we might do, he fills us with a desire for some greater good, which we shall never be able to effect. He makes this latter look exceedingly pleasant and easy, but meanwhile takes care to make us abandon altogether the first good we were doing. Then, changing his tactics, he strives to keep us from doing that other good by suddenly connecting with it some unexpected annoyance, or exaggerating the natural difficulties that attend upon it. " Your adversary, the devil, as a roaring lion, goeth about, seeking whom he may devour, whom resist ye, strong in faith." *

EXAMPLE.

THE following wonderful and instructive incident happened in the year 1665, at Siclo, in

* I. Pet. ... 8 .

Sicily, to Father Jerome Zuccaro, a priest of the
Society of Jesus:—

Afflicted with frequent attacks of epilepsy, he
lost the use of his right arm, and had almost
daily hemorrhages. As he grew worse from
day to day, he saw that he would be of little
use in the society, and therefore, as he had not
yet made his solemn profession, he decided
to ask for his dismission from the order. He
tried to write to Rome, to the Father General for that purpose — but as soon as he began
to make the effort, his left hand also became stiff
and paralyzed. He dropped his pen, but kept
to his determination of seeking a release from
his vows. Not long after this, Father Zuccaro
was planning a panegyric on St. Ignatius, and
was reading the Saint's life for that object.
Whilst thus engaged, he read of the kindness of
his holy Father towards his wavering sons. Full
of love for the holy Founder, Zuccaro ran to his
altar, and there, bursting into tears, he vowed to
St. Ignatius and to God, that however infirm,
he would remain in the Society rather than enjoy health and riches in the world. A few days
passed on after this vow, and again came another
fit of epilepsy that brought the poor man to
death's door. He then began to invoke St. Ignatius. Suddenly he beholds him before him, shin-

ing brightly, dressed in priestly robes, holding in his left hand a vase of some kind of liquid, with a twig in it, and looking very severe. With a trembling voice Zuccaro said to him: "Best of fathers ! I am your son. If you reject me, to whom can I go for help in my present danger?" The Saint answered: "I do not acknowledge as a son anyone who does not honor his father. Jerome, on account of a slight suffering you made little of the incomparable gift of vocation to a religious life." "It is so," replied Jerome; "I confess it. But you know what I have suffered. You know that I repented; you are aware of the vow by which I lately bound myself?" Then with a sweet countenance, Ignatius said: "Take courage; I shall see whether you are really my son, or no. Do you remember the formula of your vows?" Zuccaro repeated that formula, the Saint suggesting every word. "Now," said Ignatius, "I acknowledge you as my son. You are near the end of your life—you will die before sundown." "And will you allow your son to die without the Sacraments of the Church?" "Not at all. Though, by receiving viaticum and Extreme Unction, you would have gained much grace and lessened your purgatory, still the general confession, which you lately made, is sufficient to save you. However I give you your

choice. If you wish to die now, your salvation
is sure. But if you choose to prolong your life,
you must spend it in promoting the glory of
God and the salvation of souls." The sufferer
left the choice to Ignatius himself. "Choose
for me" said he, "what you know will be for God's
greater glory." "Very well, then," answered the
Saint. "You will live some time longer; God so
wills. You will recover your health, too; but
remember to use that health as becomes a son
of mine." He, then, lightly struck with the twig,
the head, hands, and feet of the patient, and
making the sign of the cross, anointed them with
the liquid from the vase, repeating as he did so,
the words: "I will strike, and I will heal."* Next
he bade him to offer up three masses, in
thanksgiving; one to the Holy Trinity, another
in honor of the Blessed Virgin, and the third
in his own honor. "For the three acts of virtue
which you have exercised in your illness," continued the Saint, "God has granted you three
graces, namely, life and health—freedom until
the hour of your death from temptations against
Chastity; but they will return, and when they
do, they will be a sign that you are about to
die. Finally God gives you the assurance that

---

* Deuteronomy, 32, v. 39.

you are predestined to eternal glory." Ignatius then held out his hand to be kissed, and giving the patient his blessing, said: " May the Lord bless you, and protect you from all evil, and lead you to everlasting life." The bystanders saw the lips of Father Zuccaro moving, but could not hear what he said. Suddenly he rose from his bed saying: "St. Ignatius has cured me." Before sunset, at which time he should have died, guns were fired, bells rang out, and there was immense festivity in the town in token of public thanks to God and to St. Ignatius.—*Bollandists for July.*

PRACTICE.

APPROACH the Sacraments of penance and the Holy Eucharist, as if you were to die immediately after their reception.

EJACULATION.

ST. IGNATIUS ! shield me from the enemy of my soul, and receive me at the hour of my death.

ASPIRATIONS

TO

ST. IGNATIUS OF LOYOLA,

Founder of the Society of Jesus.

BLESSED IGNATIUS, man of God, to whom, whilst thou wast praying, Jesus appeared, carrying his cross, and said : I will favor thee in Rome —intercede for me with that same Jesus, and beg of him to take pity on me in life, in death, and in eternity.

Holy Ignatius, who in writing thy rules and Exercises, as well as at other times, wast taught by the Blessed Virgin, from whom thou didst learn the practice of the particular examen, which thou didst teach to others, and keep up thyself until thy death, pray that I may become a good servant and a docile disciple for the Blessed Virgin and for thee.

Holy Ignatius, among the wonderful graces

which thou didst obtain from the Holy Ghost, was a great share in the cross of Christ—so that arduous and most mortifying difficulties, hostility in every form, and open persecution were thy inseparable companions during all thy life; obtain for me the grace to live on the cross, and daily to grow in conformity to Christ.

Holy Ignatius, who didst give thyself entirely to God to be used as an instrument of his glory— obtain for me, that I may always rejoice at being, until death, an instrument to serve him.

Holy Ignatius, who wast seen entering heaven at the very hour at which thou didst expire in Rome; obtain for me the happiness of entering that blessed kingdom with many titles to glory.

Holy Ignatius, who didst see thy Society covered with the mantle of the ever Blessed Virgin, obtain for me to be received under that same mantle, and to hide there forever.

Holy Ignatius, whose Society was seen by St. Teresa gloriously triumphing in heaven; obtain for me the happiness to behold and enjoy that same triumph.

Holy Ignatius, whose sons—St. Francis Xavier, the apostle of the Indies; Sts. Paul, John and

James, the first fruits of martyrdom in Japan ; St. Francis Borgia, that admirable pattern of mortification and piety; St. Francis of Hieronymo, and St. Francis Regis, men of such ardent and invincible zeal for the saving of souls ; Saints Aloysius Gonzaga and Stanislas Kostka, such wonderful examples of innocence and penance; and also the Blessed Alphonsus Rodriguez, so deep in humility, the Blessed Peter Canisius, the mallet of heretics ; the Blessed John Berchmans, so perfect a reproduction of Aloysius and Stanislas; together with so many others,—were eminent for sanctity and miracles—obtain for me, that helped by their example, I may be their not unworthy companion.

Holy Ignatius, through whom so many magnificent churches have risen to God in various parts of the world; obtain for me, who am the temple of the Holy Ghost, that I may promote the honor of God.

Holy Ignatius, who wast seen scourging the devil with a fiery scourge, when, by the lips of a possessed person, he blasphemed Christ, obtain for me grace to overcome his power as thou didst.

Holy Ignatius, who didst so often appear in glory to thy clients, who didst defend, heal and instruct them; refuse me not the help which I need at present.

Holy Ignatius, whose Exercises have been so honored by saints, so highly approved by the Holy See, and have produced so much fruit throughout the world; may that fountain of heavenly teaching never be closed to me.

Holy Ignatius, who wast healed by St. Peter appearing visibly to thee—who wast frequently visited by Jesus and Mary; whom St. Philip Neri saw shining with light, while still on earth; who didst behold the Infant Jesus under the Eucharistic Species; who didst spend eight days in ecstasy; who, while praying, was often raised from the ground, and didst hang shining in the air, and wast then heard saying: "O God ! if men knew thee ! O God ! the love of my heart;" obtain for me that similar zeal for God's glory, and a like heavenly fire may always glow in my heart, and never be quenched by earthly affections.

Holy Ignatius, who, while teaching others, didst often say with sobs, "In Christ alone, and in his cross is found true joy ; " and at another time didst say to St. Francis Xavier : "What will it benefit a man to gain the whole world, and injure his soul ?"—And again : "Conquer, conquer thyself"—impress these lessons so deeply on my mind, that I may derive from them fruits worthy of a disciple of thine.

Holy Ignatius, whom those that did not know thy name, used to call "the Father who often looks up to heaven, and speaks of God ;" draw away my mind from earthly thoughts, and fix it upon those of heaven.

Holy Ignatius, to whom the Holy Ghost appeared under the form of fire ; to whom were divinely made known the treasures hidden under the word *God*, as well as with what love and reverence that name should be used ; beg of God not to refuse to shed upon me also the light of his countenance.

Holy Ignatius, who didst praise a Sodality established under the name of Divine Love, and promise it thy assistance ; make my heart the place of assembly, as it were, of all the hearts that burn with love for God.

Holy Ignatius, who art wont to bestow on thy clients wonderful power over the devil, great success in softening obdurate hearts, ardent love for God, admirable tenderness towards the young, the sick, the scrupulous, the dying and the tempted; help me always, but chiefly at the hour of my death. Obtain for me grace to overcome myself in all things, to spend every moment of my life in such a manner that the last one, that is, the moment of my death, and all my eternity, which will then begin, may be for the honor of my great and glorious God.

Holy Ignatius, father of my soul, and worthy of all veneration from me, I beg of thee, on my knees before thee, as if I saw thee, not to cease praying to God for me, that he may grant me grace always to know his divine will with certainty, and to do it with all perfection. Amen.*

* Letters of St. Francis Xavier to St. Ignatius, Book II., Letter 9.

INVOCATIONS OF ST. IGNATIUS,

————◦✕◦————

1. ST. IGNATIUS, Founder of the Society of Jesus.—*Urban VIII., and other Pontiffs.*

2. Thou, who didst receive wonderful instruction from the Blessed Virgin, in writing the Exercises and Constitutions.—*Authors of his Life.*

3. A man whose dignity has never been sufficiently praised.—*Paramo.*

4. The father of all masters of the spiritual life.—*Ascanio Ordei.*

5. A new mirror of holiness and prudence.—*Lewis of Granada.*

6. The chief of new Apostles.–*Alvaro Piranno.*

7. Untiring opponent of heresy.—*Paramo.*

8. A great general opposed to Luther.—*Paramo.*

9. A vessel of election for the conversion of the world.—*John Chanones.*

10. A great pillar and light of the Church.—*Cardinal Paleotti.*

11. Protector of the Apostolic Roman See.—*Council of Tarragona.*

12. Successor of Paul the Apostle.—*John Chanones.* •

13. Second Captain, after the Apostles, of the bark of the Church.—*Alvaro Piranno.*

14. Apostolic giant in holiness.—*St. Francis Xavier and John of Avila.*

15. Master and leader in the faith—real martyr in a quiet life.—*Barnabites.*

16. Seventh angel of the Apocalypse veiled in

the cloud of heavenly protection.—*Council of Tarragona.*

17. Equal to the holiest patriarchs of past ages.—*Cardinal Ludovisio.*

18. In penance, another John Baptist—in obedience, Abraham.—*The same.*

19. Temple of Peace.—*Blessed John Texeda.*

20. Reviver of the world.—*Spanish Martyrology.*

21. Sun that scatters all the clouds of error.—*Council of Tarragona.*

22. Bulwark of the Christian world.—*Cardinal Ludovisio.*

23. Prop of learning and piety throughout the world.—*Council of Tarragona.*

24. General treasure of the world.—*Cardinal Ludovisio.*

25. Volcano of divine love.—*Lewis of Valentia.*

26. Man full of the Holy Ghost and of heavenly wisdom.—*Paul III.*—*Augustine Manna.*

27. Whom hell proclaimed its worst enemy.— *John Vega.*

28. Third prop of the world after St. Dominic and St. Francis.—*Dominic Grovèna, O. P.*

29. Who still produces abundant fruit all over the world by his Exercises.—*Paul III.*

30. Who was great in name—greater in saving souls—who had a soul bigger than the world.— *Gregory XIII.*

31. Who taught St. Philip Neri the art of prayer.—*St. Philip Neri.*

32. Whom the mother of God pointed out to St. Mary Magdalen of Pazzi, as a master in humility.—*St. Mary Magdalen of Pazzi.*

33. Who always spoke of God's glory, and always sought it.—*Breviary.*

34. Whose great praise it is to have for thy son, Xavier, the father of a new world.—*Breviary.*

35. Whose glory it is to have been seen in heaven as the equal of St. John Evangelist.— *St. Mary Magdalen of Passi.*

Holy Ignatius, honorable under many other titles, pray for us.

www.ingramcontent.com/pod-product-compliance
Lightning Source LLC
Chambersburg PA
CBHW030537270326
41927CB00008B/1414